T0101813

# CIDER

# CIDER

## Understanding the world of natural, fine cider

**FELIX NASH**

DOG 'n' BONE

To dad,
for all you've ever done

Originally published in 2019 as *Fine Cider*. This updated and revised edition published in 2023 by:
Dog 'n' Bone Books
An imprint of Ryland Peters & Small Ltd
20–21 Jockey's Fields      341 E 116th St
London WC1R 4BW           New York, NY 10029

www.rylandpeters.com

10 9 8 7 6 5 4 3 2 1

Editors Pete Jorgensen and Gillian Haslam
Designers: Eoghan O'Brien and Paul Stradling
Editorial director: Julia Charles
Art director: Sally Powell
Creative director: Leslie Harrington
Head of production: Patricia Harrington
Publisher: Cindy Richards

# CONTENTS

# INTRODUCTION

A few years have passed since the first edition of this book was released, and in those years cider—of the kind I talk about—has continued to steam forward. A couple of hopes I spoke about back then have started coming true, such as exquisite cider being poured by the glass at more and more restaurants across the country—no longer just the domain of the bottle or pulled pint. Likewise fine cider has been increasingly staking its claim and making itself known all over the world, with cider bars (in the style of wine bars) popping up everywhere from Paris to Portugal, and Latvia to London. I'm incredibly happy to say I have a hand in a London-based one: The London Cider House, at Borough Market, on top of those already existing in the USA.

The charming possibilities of anything new, optimistic, and exciting like this inevitably come with the associated challenges, but even with all that's been thrown at it, somehow the future of cider seems to be arriving faster and faster... For me, it's been rather a breathless pursuit, spanning most of the past decade, but I finally feel able to take a breath. And it brings me an odd joy, as a writer, to reread a conclusion to a book I previously wrote, this time through the binoculars of hindsight, and see providence made plain. But like adding fuel to any fire, a good few years have now set my mind on a path to imagining the ones that are yet to come; we've climbed a good few steps, and the view is more glorious than ever, but we are by no means at the top of the mountain...yet.

# CHAPTER 1

# The Discovery

We begin where I began—driving down the lacing lanes of the English county of Herefordshire. Situated in the middle of England, next to the Welsh border, it is a land of large, low valleys, and as you weave along its arteries you see patches of woodland, dense and dark, sat upon the hills above, with pointy pines among them. Smooth green fields rise to meet them and tuck up underneath the tree line, as though a tidal wave of trees has crested the hill and is descending toward you. Or the army in *Macbeth*, carrying trees to disguise itself, has encamped upon the hilltop, and single-file soldiers are marching down in hedgerows to the farms below.

It's a wonderful place, yet it always seems to be a lesser-known land to most of the people I meet outside of the world of cider. I've come to feel that in spite of its relative sparseness, it has a clear imprint of history upon it and an air of bygone glory lying ingrained within its existence today. It is mostly thanks to the pull of this place that I've gained a glimpse of what cider's true nature is, and all that it can be.

"All Herefordshire is become, in a manner, but one orchard," the diarist John Evelyn wrote in 1662—a person we'll come back to later. These apple trees, whose parade-ground patterns also dominate the landscape, still make up its many orchards. But today they are scattered, and pepper the view as you drive. As soon as you have an eye for an orchard, they make themselves visible everywhere; rising above or through a hedge, beyond the gap of a gate, running below a ridge, sinking into a valley. The old orchards, especially those of perry pears—the trees in which can be two or even three hundred years old—always give me a reminder of my shorter mortality as I drive by. Stood proud and ancient, versed in moss and cracking bark, they seem one of the most enduring things in the landscape.

In blossom season and when there are apples on the trees, no one can miss these orchards. Bedecked in pink and white blossom in spring, then adorned in green, yellow, and red baubles in the autumn, this landscape leaves me full of wanderlust, in wonder at all the other possible hidden pockets of the world. You can drive its lanes and bathe in its views, but it always seems to have parts that you cannot reach by road, and so holds something back from a faster pace of change.

We are here to visit Tom Oliver. Widely regarded as one of the great cider-makers of the world, he is a charming soul, so kind with his time and his belief. You find him at a farm down a short track in central Herefordshire. I have visited many times and the sensations of arriving are always the same: from the fast, smooth run of the main road you begin to slow and to indicate, with the traffic approaching behind you beginning to condense, you turn over the little lip that marks the start of the track, and your smooth and fast journey changes to wobbling and slow. Now moving sideways as well as forward, you descend the broken tarmac, avenued by young trees, toward the farm buildings at the base of the slope, sat proud among a moat of fields. I look forward to that change in texture. It signals that you have arrived at Oliver's.

From the track, you spy across the rooftops and the structure of it all, and as you pass the Hereford cattle and the last of the lane hooks you to the right, you cross the threshold through the gate into the farm itself.

↑ One of the barrel rooms at Tom Oliver's cidery.

There were hop kilns on the far side, dating from the time that Tom's granddad majored in hop growing. This was part of the reason Tom set about making the cider he does, kindled by memories of cider in his youth and the desire to return such cider-making to the farm once more.

I remember the first time I saw Tom's barrel rooms, the sharp-angled sun cutting its blades through slatted wooden sides, the breeze meandering in. Those dormant shapes of slumbering barrels, unmoved while they work, and working for years at a time. Row upon row of differing forms, different styles of barrel, from varying origins, formerly used for wine, rum, whisky, all sorts.

In this place you are aware that you are in something else's territory. It is the kingdom of wild yeasts. It's not a place made for people, but for process. Some magical, crypt-like chamber of monotone makeup, but with gold lying in its bowels. Held in a prison of steel strapping, their bulbous timber forms look built to burst, calling out to release the liquid these barrels contain and have its charms be known by the world. Or ready to take the strain and hold their burden longer, knowing the reward is worth it. Barrels are things of true tension and suspense, and yet all of this tension comes together to give a dormancy, a wait from which good things come.

Back outside, away from this slumbering room, the sun is not slatted but in full laminating form. It always seems to be sunny, or at least two steps more southern in weather in this immediate area, with a little pocket of blue sky in the clouds above, even when deep grays form a heavy roof to the surround. Perhaps my timing has just been lucky, or my memories have been altered by the cider. Either way, on this visit Tom and I pull a bench out into the sun; it is such a nice day that we wouldn't have been giving life its due savor had we not.

The image on the right is from this moment, which for me marks an early stage in the discovery of this somewhat lost world, a point of no return, that pulled me wonderfully away from what I had thought cider to be. It is my knee to the right of the image, and my hand on the bottle being poured. Between pours and sips I was sat with the sun

↑ The "first taste" at Tom Oliver's cider house.

making my eyelids orange, my face angled in the direction of its nurture, neck extended, like a flower following the light. It's a dusty track that runs through the farm, with hops growing on the hedge behind and a pear tree growing to the side of our seat. If you were to sit here, you would see red brick and timber-slatted buildings in front of you, the cider house itself.

I have come with a few blocks of cheese in my pocket, wrapped in wax paper, to soften and savor the moment of the business being done. We open and taste the first cider I ever sold. It was the first cider I produced with Tom; in fact it was the first I did with anyone—although I had no hand in its making, I simply helped choose it and the bottles it went in. But this was the first time we had tasted the end result together, and for me that was the start, sat in the sun, on that simple bench.

How to try and describe its taste? It's not simply a case of describing it compared to other tastes of well-known foods and flavors. It's hard to adequately do any justice by saying it had "notes of this, and that..." unless you've tasted much cider beyond that which fills the mass market. It had depth, and a character of its own not precisely like any other cider I have tasted since; while some might be similar, none has seemed the same. I had the whole experience there in front of me, that fullest pleasure of drinking a thing in the place of its making, with its maker, under the sun that saw its apples grow across the previous summer. Like some quiet corner in a grand cathedral, it was musky and smoky and vast, created by a craftsman in praise of a higher ideal.

# MY FIRST CIDER-MAKING VENTURE

Tom Oliver lives and works in the joyously named hamlet of Ocle Pychard—a name that seems designed to entertain what few visitors it receives. But the names of the villages and hamlets en route to his cider house start to sound familiar as they crop up in the names of apple and pear varieties. The more varieties you come to know, the more connections you make. Aylton is 8 miles away, home of the Aylton Red pear. Another 8 miles away is Catley, home of the Catley Red. Less than 4 miles away is Eggleton, the birthplace of the Eggleton Styre, while 12 miles away in the village of Much Marcle is Gregg's Pit, home to the Gregg's Pit pear, with the mother tree—the first ever of the variety—still standing today, more than 200 years old, and under the care of the wonderful cider- and perry-maker, James Marsden. The same village holds a house called Hellens, one of the oldest dwellings in England and with three pear varieties that are apparently native to its driveway.

If such distances show the locality that apples and pears can have, and hint at just how varied they might be, so too do Tom's ciders show the vibrancy and depth that cider itself can hold. And it was under his wing that I first learnt what the view looks like from up on the highest heights. Tom is a passioned man, one so very aware of reality and as such so very able to act as its steward. Working to the greatest complexities wild yeasts allow, his slowly fermenting subconscious pushes the boundaries, trialing, testing, and modeling steps forward in his mind.

Tom works with the most wonderful tools, as he walks the fine line afforded by wild yeasts (see page 128), between getting as much from that specific apple or blend or individual fermentation as possible, and letting the cider stray into undesired territory. For embracing wild yeasts holds greater risk; more avenues can open for faults to develop, but the rewards can also be greater: far more layered and far more vibrant.

While this was our first taste together, this was not the first taste of this specific cider for me; the first taste was a far less relaxing experience. Through the quirks of minor technical obstacles, it was bottled at Pershore Agricultural College, across the border from Herefordshire in Worcestershire (that most charming of places to hear an American try to pronounce!).

↑ Tom Oliver.

I had bought the bottles (1,834 bottles per pallet still sticks in the mind), and the labels were designed by friends, the talented Seb White and Eva Kellenberger. So it was that in Pershore, at 9am on a Wednesday, I got my first taste of that cider; a single-variety cider made with the Yarlington Mill apple. I remember it tasted terrible. Fear ran through my body as my mind reacted to the horror of a future crumbling; all my efforts and hopes of recent months crumpled into a little black hole in the middle of my mind. And then I realized that the last thing I had done that morning was to brush my teeth; for those of you who know the combination of orange juice and toothpaste, the effect is no less pronounced. Toothpaste suppresses the receptors in your taste buds that detect sweet flavors, with the effect of heightened bitterness. Add to that the expectation I had of the cider I was tasting, having tasted it from the tank before bottling, and it made for a very a heavy moment.

In spite of the terror that toothpaste brought, that very same cider went on to be a benchmark—tasting exquisite later in the day when the toothpaste had fully washed away, and going on to win first prize for the best single-variety cider at the International Cider and Perry Competition 2014, at the Hereford Cider Museum.

The few thousand bottles I had were loaded in large fruit packaging crates, like shipping pallets with wooden sides. At bottling we had no boxes in which to house them, as they had not arrived in time, so these crates were the only option. I remember the feeling of riches, lifting their cardboard lids to see the shining gold laid down inside, such was the glow the cider gave. So I set about, driving for three days, to London and back, to London and back, to London and back; and on reaching our yard the first time, full of relief, closing the large black metal gates and going out onto the street in search of someone with a forklift truck. It was easier than I had feared; at first I found a guy from a fabric wholesaler up the road and gave him a tiny bit of cash to fork these crates from the van. Then I discovered the friendly chaps at the printers a little less up the road, in particular a guy named Marcus, who I still see today, stood outside the printers, soaking up the world. We chat about how business is going and how the area is changing. I would give him a bottle or two, in thanks for his help. With the first 7,000 labels then applied by hand, by myself, by friends, and by family, I set out to see how they would be received in the bars and restaurants of London.

In the half decade since, things have come a long way, both in what I do and in the wider world of cider. Gone are the days of such tasks as buying empty bottles; instead myself and others ply our trade as cider merchants; like wine merchants, but solely stocking and supplying cider and perry, digging in hopefully ever-greater depths into the ciders created each season, finding those which seem something special. We began with London, but now supply across the whole of the UK mainland, mostly to wholesale customers but increasingly to the public, too. But from that first experience, with the toothpaste, I learnt an important lesson: to be cautious and to taste things more than once, as where you are and what you last ate or drank can change how something tastes.

I wouldn't say that I wound up here, doing what I do now, through any specific intention. It was something a little simpler, yet no less inexorable than

→ Bottles of Oliver's cider.

that, like some sort of gravity. I took the first steps off the beaten path and was drawn slowly ever farther in. But I would also say to remember that these are my eyes, what I see. I have an imagination but it's based fundamentally on the reality I have found, and as with anything you can only speak with the eyes of your own experience, as you interpret it. I am not purporting to report on the world of cider as a whole, nor not acknowledge that cider, as with any form of taste, is a most subjective thing. So I will focus less on how the ciders I speak of taste, and more on how they are made and why this makes a difference. If you agree with me, great; if not, that's absolutely fine. Dig into things through your own eyes and add what you find to the world. The world is vast enough. If you feel you do not know enough to either agree or disagree, even better! For you can set about discovering for yourself, with the pages of this book as a bouncing board off which your experiences may spring. Like a wonderful movie that can only be seen with fullest impact the first time, you have it all at your feet, you have that greatest pleasure of all, the uniquely personal charms of self-discovery, waiting for only you.

And also note that I know that while I have engaged above all with the world of fine cider here in Britain, I'll touch on other parts of the world, but would be doing them a disservice to pretend I know them in the way I know my own. From America we have the voices of others, those doing and knowing some of the most wonderful goings-on there, to help fill this void (see pages 114–118). And, for other regions, I will not go to anywhere near such depth as I would not do them justice, but look forward to reading whole other books that might.

# THE ROLE OF THE POMMELIER

A pommelier is for cider what a sommelier is for wine. If the sommelier is a "steward of wine," who holds an in-depth understanding of wine, and is needed because there is much to know and so many bottles to choose between. The role of the pommelier is in itself a reflection on the similarities that wine and cider at their peak can hold. We work closely with customers to choose their cider list. For cider is not brewed like beer, but made, as is wine. You are not heating and combining multiple ingredients, but taking the juice of a fruit and fermenting its fruit sugars into alcohol. As such, the ciders of the kind I am speaking about will vary each year, even when made by the same maker and in the same manner. How they turn out will depend on the weather of the season and the way this affects the apples as they grow. And even once made into cider and put in a bottle, the cider will still change over time as it ages.

There were, of course, some first fascinating bottles that I tasted, those that really bit and have never let go, wonderfully infecting me to this day. But getting to know a view of the fuller map of the finer side of cider did take its time. One of the first occasions that I got to really sample a taste map of many ciders and perries in one go, to see how nuanced the contours were, was at the Putley Trials, in the village of Putley in Herefordshire. It is a closed-door competition, but is part of a wider array of public events called the Big Apple, arranged by a wonderful group of devotees.

It was a hot day in early May. In a small village hall with the windows open, we tasted some 60 or 70 ciders and perries. In the wine world everyone would likely be spitting after tasting, but here a little less so. If we liked a cider we would finish the tiny sample in our glass; if not, there were buckets, or easier still, an open window through which to throw it. I remember the perries made with the Thorn perry pear, from the latest season and so only seven or eight months old, were particularly wonderful that year, winning many awards. For the first time I got a view of how exquisite a single variety alone could be, and how high the heights were. And so beyond it, to the wider landscape your curiosity turns; what will the weather that season allow to ascend to such vintage heights, what are the other highest peaks like, where in the world can you travel to find similar things!

→ Me, in an orchard, cider in belly and hand.

# LEARNING THE BUSINESS

I didn't know much about cider when I started my business, and had little experience in wine, or food, or sales, or wholesale. I had the joy of growing up in the age of the arrival of the Internet, and I could gain a little insight into so much of what was new to me via Google, such is the custom of the Internet age. But I also thought this uninitiated perspective might not be such a negative, perhaps it could even be a positive. Why not start from the beginning, from first principles, as perhaps coming at things with an outsider's view can leave you unburdened by the existing norms? You can think a little more freely, rather than simply through the eyes of the collective conscious, and some of what you discover will have (perhaps) a more grounded foundation.

It's very hard to know much about cider—there are the odd (in both senses of the word) books here and there, but I feel few show cider as I know it. Of course, there are many objective things, things that are little known but irrefutable and fascinating, things that seen with fresh eyes are so valuable, when plucked from history and placed in the right hands. Ways of thinking about and of making cider, that fuel and are fueled by a different aspiration to the norm of the mass market today. Such is the way of looking that I see in many of the best cider-makers I encounter. The best cider is not yet well enough known for many of these makers' creations to be judged on established tenets. The gulf between the ends of the cider spectrum is huge, and it's a hard gorge to leap, getting ever wider the better your view of the far side becomes. And so many ciders and written accounts already out there should be approached with that hardest of things to know: the gaps, the flaws, the industrial background, and so on.

I know a fair bit now; I can sit for hours speaking very quickly at a saturated sommelier or restaurateur, reeling off information, anecdotes, points of understanding on all that cider was, is, and I think can be. Such monologues can be a rambling array of all things soaked in; choice snippet and golden nugget found in otherwise lifeless books, or old books made wonderfully accessible thanks to Google Books, that otherwise I would

↑ A maker's selection at a Fine Cider tasting.

never have found. But most of it comes from the makers themselves, discussions and conversations over the past years; and in the true nature of knowledge, the main thing I now know is just how much there might be that I don't know…

Over the last few years I have witnessed what's been referred to as the New Wave: new cider-makers, many of them young, making without the shackles of previous thinking. Not caught in the middle, not halfway there; not held back by the old tropes, but completely free to make cider entirely as they wish, often taking influence from the world of wine and taking the orchards, the apples, the methods that they work with to their greatest potential. The finer end of the cider spectrum is a thing still being written; it is a newly emerging world. The charting of its boundaries and borders, the key characters, and the values its citizens hold dearest are all in their infancy.

I have the privilege of doing what I can to connect the creations of this New-Wave world to the restaurants, bars, bottle shops, wine merchants, delicatessens, and other establishments of my country. From those tentative early days, where there was much to test and prove, I now have the joy in that pinch-yourself manner of finding myself sat at the bar and tables of the most wonderful places, with some incredibly talented people I can call customers. It is a testament to cider itself. Today we work with three or four restaurants in the UK which feature in *The World's 50 Best Restaurants* list, and find cider a fit on the bar menus and wine lists of the iconic, such as The Fat Duck and L'Enclume, as well as the more recently emerged beacons of brilliance, such as Lyle's (see page 175), the Clove Club, and Carters of Moseley.

Much of the challenge is simply letting people know that something they have not encountered before exists, as the quality of the cider so often speaks for itself. And that perpetually raises the question of what formulates the perceptions that people have, in this case what cider is. To what extent is it objective elements, and to what extent is it reputation in the public eye? What is quality, in a thing little known, and so judged by a smaller rather than wider world? I've spent a lot of time thinking about these questions, but I've also got to know the world from which the ciders I work with come, and some of the greatest pleasure and fascination is simply spending time with the cider-makers themselves, discovering the landscapes, localities, and lives in which they work. Such as visiting the tithe barn that cider-makers James and Susanna Forbes, of Little Pomona Cidery in Herefordshire, have been using for their "Champagne (or traditional) Method" cider. It is an ancient place, guarded by a huge Great Dane that is nearly blind and barks vehemently as you arrive, as though it is guarding some ancestral treasure. With its wattled wooden sides, the barn allows large dots of bright light in

through its gaps, sitting like shining gold coins, speckling those precious bottles as they sit on their pupitres (the wooden stands used in the Method). Or aboard a boat in Devon with Polly and Mat of Find & Foster (see page 152), sipping their cider at a 40-degree angle as we sail to a pub that can't be reached by road, only boat, bike, or foot, to eat seafood that landed at a shore only a mile or so away. To then slowly sail back afterward, in ever-nearing darkness, bellies beholden to their filling, as a huge tipsy yellow moon rises like a mushroom behind the naval academy on the far shore.

← Cider at Lyle's.

# WHAT IS CIDER?

But what is cider? Or to give it its American name, *hard cider* (to keep things simple, I will simply call it cider in this book). A very basic description would be: the juice of apples, some of the fruit sugars of which have been fermented to alcohol by yeasts. The reality of what can legally be called "cider" is a slightly different thing, and we will get into this later. The apples used to make cider can be any, but there are certain apple varieties that have historically been chosen and prized particularly for cider-making, and they are known as cider apples. Often they will not be eaten or cooked, and will solely be grown and used for cider as the properties which make them wonderful for cider-making often make them near unpalatable to eat. They tend to have high levels of sugar, so you might assume they'd taste sweet, but they also have high levels of bitterness and astringency that are often more prominent than this sugar, so the taste you perceive can be incredibly bitter and unpleasing, compared to the sweetness of most eating apples.

The yeasts that do the fermenting can be wild—those naturally present in the apples and the ambient environment—or they can be what are called "inoculated yeasts" or "cultured yeasts," which are really best thought of as laboratory yeasts, as they are predominantly wild yeast strains that have been chosen for their properties and potency, isolated in a lab and bred in their billions and trillions. Usually freeze-dried and arriving in a packet, they will often dominate a fermentation; they are usually only one strain of yeast and highly potent. For more on yeast, see pages 128–131. But as cider begins with apples, so shall we.

→ Tasting cider before it is released.

# APPLE VARIETIES

There are thousands of apple varieties in the world; I've often heard it mentioned in the cider world that there are over 7,000 apple varieties, perhaps 10,000 or more. But categorically, in the 19th century there were around 14,000 documented varieties growing in the northeast of the United States alone. This roughly accounts for different names given to the same varieties, without which the number recorded was some 17,000. Yet today only around 90 or 100 apple varieties are commercially grown in the USA. In Russia, there are said to be as many as 6,000 cultivars (apples cultivated in some way by the actions of man, rather than occurring naturally in the wild), and there are an estimated 20,000 named cultivars across the wider world, so it seems for once the hearsay likely underestimated things.

Some 2,500 or so distinct cultivars are thought to exist in Britain; and even today more than 2,000 different named apple varieties can be found growing at the National Apple Collection at Brogdale, in Kent. I've heard of there having once been a little over 350 named cider apple varieties being grown in Britain, at a time not historically specified, as well as some 500+ varieties of cider apple in the north of France. And a recent report, published in 2018, listed some 101 apple and pear varieties native to Wales, 73 of them supposedly new discoveries or rediscoveries.

Why do so many apple varieties exist? And why is the exact number not more certain and seemingly so variable across time? It's down to the nature of how apples reproduce. For if you take the seed of an apple, plant it in the ground, and get it to grow, when this tree matures and creates apples they will not be identical to the apple from which you got the seed; they will not be genetically the same, nor will they taste exactly the same. A little like the reproduction of many things, humans included, the result will not exactly mirror its parents. Apple trees do not reproduce true to type, as the blossom of most apple trees cannot self-pollinate, and so the pollen of a different variety is required for them to pollinate. The apples that grow on the tree itself will be the same year after year, but the seeds these apples contain will

↑ Apples are abundant things.

all vary, being a genetic cross between the two parents.

It makes me wonder each time I see miscellaneous apple trees growing wild in hedgerows along country lanes, or on the verges of roads—what could it be that has grown from a seed, a rare example of something from which exquisite cider could be made? That chance creation by genetic variation of a variety we find wonderful for the finest cider? The chance, while slim, exists and is fascinating to consider, as is which varieties may have existed in the past, or may come to exist in the future.

# APPLE CULTIVATION

When you find a variety that makes wonderful cider, how do you grow more of it if you can't simply plant the seeds and grow more trees? How do you take a wonderful cider apple, prized for its properties, and turn it into an orchard? For this you must use the arts of grafting and budding. You can think of these a little like cloning. There are a number of slight variations in precisely how you can do it, but basically you are taking genetic material from the tree that grows the apples you wish to replicate, and you apply this genetic information to a host, and in turn that grows to produce more of the same apples.

Usually this means cutting buds or graftwood from the desired tree (buds that will otherwise turn into the blossom which, when pollinated, creates the fruit), and attaching them to the host tree, in such a way that they bond and grow together as one. The genetics of the host tree will still define the apples that grow from any branches originating from the host tree, but any branches that grow from this graft or bud will hold the variety you desire.

The graft or bud is often called scion wood; one of the definitions of scion is "a descendent of a notable family," and to attach it to the host involves

making a cut in the host tree to expose the layers beneath the bark, which is put in contact with the exposed cut part of the graft or bud. You can attach more than one variety onto a single tree; famously there is an apple tree in Sussex that has around 250 different apple varieties growing on it. But if, as is usually done, you begin with the smallest beginnings of a tree rather than one that is fully grown, and make sure that this host tree only forms the roots or stem of the tree, and the desired variety forms all the branches, then you will get solely the desired apples growing on the

← A branch growing from the rootstock (or the "host tree") will not produce the desired apple variety.

tree. And as such, a new tree with the desired apples is born. This host tree that forms the roots and stem is called the rootstock. It will be a variety chosen for its strong roots, its resistance to rot, etc., and it defines how big the tree will become. Sometimes the stem will not be a part of it, as on many occasions a different variety is chosen and forms what is called the interstem, above the roots but below the branches. So an apple tree will often be made up of two or three different apple varieties, joined and growing together like some Frankenstein plant.

↑ A very obvious graft mark on a tree.

It seems rather mad that you can do this, and that it works as well as it does. To be sure, it is a skillful thing to do successfully (even the best surgeon in the world cannot take a finger from one patient and have it grow into a whole arm on someone else).

You can often see the graft mark on trees, with a distinct line cutting across the bark at these divides. Some are very obvious—for example, the Thorn perry pear, which forms a large bulbous shape above the graft line. Once you know of it, seemingly indistinguishable perry pear trees separate themselves out, and such differences really stand out.

It is because the seeds of an apple will not be true to the apple they came from, and a variety must be grafted for new trees to have the same fruit, that so many apple varieties exist; variety is built into the apple's nature. This also means there is a first-ever tree for each apple variety that comes into existence, called the mother tree. For example, there is a garden in Nottinghamshire that has the first Bramley apple tree, dating from 1809. Incredibly it is over 200 years old, but apparently seems to be dying. And a garden in New South Wales holds the first Granny Smith apple tree, dating from 1868.

Apple trees are hermaphrodites, carrying both sexes in their flowers, yet almost all are unable to fertilize themselves; in Britain there are apparently only around three varieties that can successfully self-pollinate and grow fruit. So in many modern orchards you see other apple tree varieties, often planted individually and interspersed in the rows, in order to ensure successful pollination. Thought might also be given to which varieties are planted, such that one can pollinate the other, if these interspersed individual trees are not added.

# THE ORIGIN OF APPLES

Most of the apples we come across today are known as the domestic or sweet apple. The scientific name is *Malus pumila*, but at times they are (apparently incorrectly, according to the rules of botanical nomenclature) referred to as *Malus domestica*. Nonetheless, they can be thought of as domesticated apples. Wild European crab apples—*Malus sylvestris*—are something different, they grew in Europe before the advent of farming and were found in woodlands and grassland. So how did these domesticated apples come into existence, and why are they so prominent over wild crab apples today? Well, if you think of animals, from the pets we have at home to the wild animals of the Earth, not all have been domesticated, nor necessarily can be. Those animals that have been domesticated (such as cats and dogs) exist in great abundance and have often changed a lot from their wild ancestors. A similar thing is true for apples.

Those apple varieties that have been domesticated are called "cultivars," meaning varieties that have been cultivated: promoted in growth by the attention of humans in some way, at some stage. The ahead-of-his-time Russian botanist and geneticist Nikolai Vavilov put forth a theory as to the origins of the domesticated apple in the first half of the 20th century, suggesting that its ancestors were the wild apples (*Malus sieversii*) of the Tien Shan in central Asia, and DNA evidence collected over the past decades does support the bulk of his theory.

The Tien Shan is a large mountain range, spanning some 1,000 miles from Uzbekistan to western China. There are huge mountains in this range, the highest being 24,406 ft (7,439m) high. They formed 10–12 million years ago, and are still rising, increasing in height by as much as ½ in (1.5cm) a year. The forests of wild fruit trees that sit far below these peaks extend from Kazakhstan to the shores of the Black Sea in eastern Europe, and apples aren't the only fruit—others, such as plums and nuts, are also found growing here. But the Tien Shan is of particular note for apples, with whole

↑ The Tien Shan mountain range.

hillsides and valleys dominated by apple trees; up to 80 percent of the density in parts of these fruit forests can be apple trees.

Back in the 1990s Nikolai Vavilov wrote that all around the city of Almaty (the largest city in Kazakhstan, and the new name for the region of Alma Ata, meaning Full of Apples or City of Apples) could be seen a vast expanse of wild apples in the mountains. Wild *Malus pumila* can still be found in a few isolated pockets of forest, and it seems that when wild apple trees first arrived in the region they spread along riverbanks and mountain chains, making the most of these humid enclaves.

I have often noticed that perry pear trees in particular tend to have very stocky stems connecting the pears to the tree, and always presumed that this is simply to be strong enough to bear the fruit—indeed, for anyone who has seen how heavily laden an apple tree can be (almost more apple than tree in the most extreme). But it seems the size of the stems also played another role: longer, more flexible stems allow the fruit to move in strong winds, and this apparently makes such varieties more prone to being distributed by birds, who can perch on the stems to eat the fruit. The shorter stems of *Malus pumila* apples being less suited for birds, presumably made their dispersal slightly more orientated toward other animals, particularly the presumably shorter range of land animals. There is a theory that the mountain peaks of the Tien Shan trapped these early apples for a while, so they developed as they have in the region, but once a few scout-like seedlings made it over these peaks to the west they found large amounts of fitting habitat, spreading their way across much of the temperate regions of the northern hemisphere.

Where did these early wild ancestors come to the Tien Shan from? It's likely they derive from southern China, partly due to the fact that central and southern China is said to be the place of the richest diversity of species within the *Malus* genus. Supposedly, plant species spread around the globe, finding new places to call home, quicker than animals do. But combine this with the last 10,000–12,000 years since agriculture developed and the precise origins of the domestic apple are hard to know for certain.

The effect and interaction that humans have had with apples is a complex, long-running subject, which does blur the boundaries between wild and cultivated species. But 3,500–5,500 years ago, long-distance trading began to blossom, with the rise of city states and trade routes running from the Mediterranean through to present-day Pakistan. The forests of the Tien Shan lie at the heart of these trading routes, the wider region known as the "wild fruit belt," and the spread of the apple began. You can imagine the apple advancing across centuries, from eaten and transported apples growing into trees—by birds, bears, horses, other animals, and people.

As such we start to see apples appear in the written record. It was purported that pharaoh Rameses II planted apple trees along the banks of the Nile in the 13th century BC, but this is disputed, and in *Odyssey*, the Greek poet Homer, writing at around the 8th century BC, tells of a large orchard. In ancient Greece, the apple gained notoriety, appearing as one of the *Twelve Labours of Hercules*, where he had to steal the golden apples of the Hesperides (the nymphs of evening and of sunset's golden light); from a garden guarded by a dragon, often depicted as a snake—not unlike another famous tale we know.

# THE SPREAD IN EUROPE

In the Middle Ages, the majority of apples grown in Europe were used for cider-making, while in England cider battled ale for dominance as the most-drunk drink. As well as the wealth of the landed gentry a good few centuries later, the wealth in lands and labor of religion was a world in which orchards could flourish. Following the Norman Conquest of Britain in 1066 Europe and England became more closely intertwined; across the following century or so Cistercian monks spread far and wide, bringing with them their practice of cultivating the land of their abbeys with emphatic vigor. Long after the Romans left the shores of Britain, orcharding found a context in which it could again take hold in Britain. It seems the monks were skillful cider-makers, bringing their wine-making knowledge to bear. Cider played an ingrained role for some churches at the time, with 74 of 80 parishes in West Sussex in 1341 paying tithes to the church in cider.

As the Renaissance arrived, Italy saw the return of an appreciation of the apple. Inspired by the Romans before them, the love and appreciation of fresh fruit boomed, with the trading might of Venice building lavish palaces, and the patronage of artists such as Botticelli leading to exquisite works of art, especially still-life works of sumptuous arrays of fruit. Such fruit was not

→ The Romans are credited with the early spread of orchards in Europe.

↑ ← ↓ There is a vast number of different varieties of apples and pears, spread across the globe. They can have all sorts of beautiful colors, markings and tastes.

just treated as food but as pageantry; it was a costly luxury. Having fresh fruit on your table was a symbol of status; a little like the owning or renting of a pineapple in 18th-century England (this rare and exotic fruit, discovered by Columbus a few centuries before, was a symbol of wealth and power). As was so often the case, the aristocracy followed the example of royalty, and such an appreciation of fresh fruit spread to France and on to England.

The Reformation and King Henry VIII's split from the Catholic church in the 16th century saw the confiscation of the lands of the Cistercian abbeys in England. But their removal left the door open to the landed gentry, who followed the example of Henry's fruiterer in cultivating orchards. Momentum grew during the reigns of King James I and King Charles I, and the cultivation of different varieties, the naming of them, and the prizing of the best became a cherished pursuit. Even the King on a trip to Hereford was recalled to favor the cider of the region: "both King, Nobility and Gentry, did prefer it before the beft wines thofe parts afforded." Fine cider-making was a pursuit of the wealthy, those with the ability to engage in such luxuries, producing literature and advice, advancing orchards and cider-making respectively.

From here the apple and cider-making spread, out to America with the Protestant settlers as they landed on the eastern seaboard of what is now the United States, and across to the west as they worked their way inland, eventually reaching the Pacific Coast. Grain was precious for these settlers, and so beer was made less often, yet apple trees could be grown on ground such crops could not, and did well when left relatively to their own devices. In this era traders also took the first apple trees to Australia and South Africa, and both regions remain notable apple-growing and cider-making regions today. So the dominance of the apple orchard was established; it had conquered the globe, traveling by virtue of empires and traders, while they themselves conquered the globe. The domestic apple, far from its Asiatic home, had ingrained itself in the cultures of the Western powers and their dominions.

# CHAPTER 2

# Cider, from Past to Present

The history of cider is formed by the origin of apple species: the very nature of this fruit and how it spread across the world. The thriving of the fittest apples in the eyes of man, by the hand of man, where nature would allow. Yet the element of the hand of the individual is a thing we often overplay. Discoveries often have unintended, if at times wonderful, consequences—predominantly other unintended discoveries—and the world of alcohol is no different.

In the world of Champagne for example, the myth of Dom Pérignon as the inventor of Champagne serves well for marketing. But the reality is this is simply not true. The invention of Champagne as we know it, and the refinement of the Champagne Method (see page 148), spanned some 200 years, and evolved with the input of many, often people who were not the wine-makers themselves. But more to the point, when we look into the very origins of Champagne, we will also learn something fascinating about the history of cider.

Cider-making has evolved in complexity since it was first discovered, and the understanding and techniques applied to it—from the manipulation and use of trees, orchards, and apples, to the actual process of making cider—are now vastly complex and have spanned centuries. Small and subtle variations, tests, experiments, and happy accidents have spread the branches of the family tree of cider-making far and wide. The techniques used have grown, and been shared to become greater than the sum of their parts. They are applied each season by cider-makers across the world, and are the fruit of this family tree, as it grows another season older and more complex. Some branches have died and been lost, while others have been on the verge of disappearing, with but a few leaves left alive on their limbs.

↓ Cows graze in an orchard. Polyculture has historically been a part of cider-making.

# MAKING CIDER

The simple matter of effort seems to shape much of the history of both cider and alcohol as a whole; from ancient methods to the machinery of today, it shapes the cost in time and now in money that a thing takes to make. The key to early alcohol-making would have been the acquiring of liquid with sugar in it, such that the sugar could ferment into alcohol. Mead, for example, also known as honey wine, is likely an ancient drink; combine honey from wild bee hives with water and you have a liquid from which alcohol can be made. You might risk being stung by bees to get the honey, but both exist naturally as liquids, so no juicing is required.

The apple itself and cider are two separate (if inseparable) things. Overall cider is likely not as old as many would assume, precisely because of the effort it takes to make. It might seem a very traditional drink, being made in what would seem very old-fashioned, even timeless ways, to the delight of tourists passing farms in the west of England. But in all likelihood it has only been made in any sort of large quantities within the past few thousand years. Like so many things, how long cider-making has existed at any scale, and how it has been made since its discovery, is defined by relatively subtle factors, across vast swathes of time; for apples this quite simply comes down to how strong they are. Grapes are soft fruit, you can press them with your feet, but apples you can't. So in some ways, this makes wine actually easier to make than cider. To juice an apple, to break the cell walls within it and allow the juice to run free, is not such an effortless task. Even today, to press whole apples is an inefficient task and requires vast amounts of pressure. It is far easier if you grind up the apple, and then press this ground-up apple.

This grinding is called milling, and it takes technology to do. Once ground, the apple is known as pulp. Originally this was as simple as the principle of using a large pestle and mortar, and then pounding the apples in a trough—a hollowed-out tree trunk combined with a large stick made for a good such tool. It would have been inefficient, and you can imagine how much effort it would have taken. So later, hand and horsepower (just 1hp) were employed to turn big, circular grinding wheels, crushing the apples in a large circular trough as it was pulled in circles. Many remnants of these old mills can still be found across Herefordshire today, as they were once in widespread use, but now they tend to be sat in gardens or farmyards, often moss-covered and with their wooden parts long rotted away.

↑ An old mill stone at Gregg's Pit in Herefordshire.

You needed a hard stone to make such a mill, such as granite, or in Herefordshire, Forest of Dean stone from nearby Gloucestershire was often used. The stone had to be heavy to press the fruit, and hardy to last without cracking, so it was quite an investment, costing some £20 or £30 all told, around US$6,000–8,500 (£4,500–6,500) in today's money. They are similar to the mills used in Greek and Roman times for pressing olives for oil, but where the mills for olives were made to not crush the stones in the olives, the mills for apples would usually have only one wheel, and would apply the full weight of the stone when milling.

However, this wasn't the only method. Supposedly in Germany, apples were traditionally grated by hand, rather than crushed. And eventually, and to this day, spinning blades or crushing metal rollers replaced stone and became the norm. One of the first such devices was Worlidge's Ingenio, and the mechanization of the Industrial Revolution tolled the death knell to the role of the horse in yet another industry. Unlike the heavy stone mills, such devices were portable and could be operated by a single person.

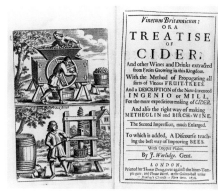

← Drawing of Worlidge's Ingenio.

# PRESSING APPLES

Grinding the apples is only the first stage; the second is actually pressing them. And since we have run a course through a brief history of grinding, we have to go back in time again. While the pestle-and-mortar approach would have served both purposes—crushing and juicing the apples in one go, albeit very inefficiently—things changed after the Romans invaded Britain in the 1st century AD, as they brought with them large wooden presses for making wine. These presses used the power of the screw, or leverage generated by a long, weighted or pressured wooden beam. Huge contraptions, the large timber beams alone could weigh half a ton or more, they could press a large amount in one go. Many smaller presses to this day work by the same principles: layers of ground apple pulp are wrapped in cloths, usually in a rectangular shape, and these rectangles are assembled atop each other. Originally straw would have been used as the wrapping, allowing the flexibility required for pressing, but still providing enough structure to keep things together when the pressure was applied.

A whole new realm of efficiency opened up thanks to this Roman import to Britain, perhaps securing with it the affinity Britain holds with cider. Some cider-makers still press through straw in this manner, but this is mostly now a novelty. I came across a maker in Cornwall, upon whose farm cider has supposedly been made since the 13th century, and where they still press through straw. Nowadays most small cider-makers that press in this manner use cloths made of a synthetic material and a hydraulic press, and such machines make things far easier and more efficient.

There are many different kinds of apple presses on the market, but for me the process of milling and pressing is not so interesting: you are simply getting the juice from the apple, and as far as quality goes there are many more important factors, such as the apples you choose to press, how and where they were grown, and ultimately what you do with the juice once you

↑ Forest of Dean stone press.

have freed it from the cellular embrace of the apple.

There is one stage between milling your apples and pressing them for their juice that can be important, and is employed by many a wonderful cider-maker. This is called macerating: the practice of leaving the ground apples, usually for a few hours or overnight, before pressing. The ground apple interacts with the air and this can enhance the aromas of the resulting cider, as well as reducing tannin levels. There are a good number of historical

→ Cider being pressed using cloths at Gregg's Pit.

↓ Pressing cloths drying in the sun.

references to macerating, speaking of its importance in making the finest ciders. Its importance does, however, vary depending on the apples and the technique the cider-maker is using.

# THE FIRST FINE CIDERS

Things do so often change with the trends of an era, and the history of alcohol, as far as we can know it, is such a human history. So often craved and precious, of so many forms and creations, alcohol is not a new discovery by any means, but it is certainly one that is forever changing.

The earliest evidence of wine-making goes back to 6000 or 7000 BC, and most wines were once made from dried, raisined grapes. Many wines were sour, and sweet wines the most prized. It was only toward the end of the Middle Ages that wines made from fresh grapes and fermented to dryness became truly prized in Europe. The aging of wines, a well-known thing today, only really took off from the mid-1800s, following changes in taste and technical understanding, and it was Georgian England that first came to appreciate aged dry wine.

Indeed England, and London in particular, played one of the most significant roles in the modernization of wine to what we know it as today. Wine-makers in mainland Europe had large local markets, and even the royalty and aristocracy of a nation would almost exclusively drink wine from within their borders. It makes sense, if you have much wine made close by, that that is what you drink. In England, however, following the mini ice age in the 17th and 18th centuries, viticulture had all but disappeared. London was one of the wealthiest cities on Earth at the time, and as it had few, if any, domestic wine-makers to supply it, it bought in wine from all over Europe. Without patriotic pride shaping what it desired the most, the result was that demand shaped supply, and the modern taste of wine was set in motion.

If you go even farther back to Greek and Roman times, before much of this refinement of wine, when wine was ready to drink it would have been cut with water, usually more water than wine, such as two or three parts water to wine. This was largely to do with improving the quality of the water of the time, as the wine helped sanitize it, but this addition of water was likely also to make the sour wines of the time more palatable, something that has an intriguing similarity in my mind with many of the mass-market ciders of today, where "ciders" high in alcohol are made from apple-juice concentrate and then water is added.

But it's not just the history of wine that might be unexpected or different to today: beer, for example, did not always have hops in it—they were initially added sometime between the 9th and 13th centuries AD, and primarily for their preservative properties rather than for taste.

My point? So too has cider not always been what it is today: a highly industrialized thing, homogenized and existing solely as sweet, sparkling, cheap, and poured by the pint. There have been times when the threads of the world wove in such a way that cider became much more. Prime among them is an era that is thought of as the heyday of British cider, a cultural phenomenon of finesse that saw cider elevated to a status since lost, that spanned the 17th and 18th centuries.

↑ Cider was once a very different thing to today's industrial creations.

At the time, around two centuries before Darwin was writing his most notable work, a group of gentlemen working in the field of natural philosophy—or the study of nature—founded the Royal Society in England. Widely regarded as the birth of modern science, its members would meet to share knowledge; their motto was *Nullius in verba*, meaning "On the word of no one." John Evelyn was supposedly one of those involved with coining this motto shortly after the formation of the society. Its members devoted substantial time and effort to the improvement of cider, quickly discovering that a key factor in making the best-quality cider was the choice of apples used. They tested the ciders of different apples, with attention to the best regions and their soils.

The most legendary apple variety of the era is said to have come into existence by virtue of Lord Scudamore of Holme Lacy in Herefordshire, at that time King Charles I's ambassador to France. Supposedly, having returned from France, he raised the Redstreak apple from seed. By many accounts, this apple made the best cider of all. There were two villages said to be particularly suited to the Redstreak—Holme Lacy and King's Capel in Herefordshire—and as such these two villages were said to produce some of the finest cider in the country.

The Foxwhelp apple, which is one of the oldest known cider apples around today (see page 75), supposedly derives from the Forest of Dean in

Gloucestershire, and was also said to be something superior, producing a cider with a "vinous, musky, flavor." Both fetched up to 60 or 70 times the price of common cider. But the Redstreak was king, prized above all else, being said to "excel common cider as the grape of Frontignac, Canary, or Baccharach, excels the common French grape." The Redstreak apple did apparently make it across to the United States, but likely not true to its original nature.

In the east of England, the Golden Permain is said to have been one of the most highly prized for cider; as is the case today, this part of the country did not seem to grow the same apple varieties as the west, with the Golden Permain today known as an eating apple; the cider it made was described by some as weak in comparison to other ciders of the time.

We cannot know what these ciders truly tasted like, just as we cannot truly know the tastes of the time by which to judge their descriptions. But the cider seemed to go down well, with some 5,500 liters (1,452 gallons) of cider being drunk at Lord Scudamore's Christmas celebrations in 1639 alone. And John Evelyn reported a blind tasting, the result of a bet, pitting the cider of a Herefordshire cider-maker against the best wines of a London vintner, the hands-down winner of which was the Redstreak cider.

Perhaps one of the best testaments to how cider was seen by some at the time was the emergence of the cider flute. The Cider Museum in Hereford has a collection of them, hailing from the 18th century. Made from lead crystal glass, they are exquisitely ornate things, etched and engraved. One of the most famous of such cider flutes is in the Museum of London and was one of the flutes of Lord Scudamore, and has the most decorative adornment. And the subject of glass brings us to another discovery of the time.

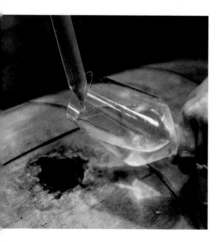

← Sampling directly from the barrel.

# THE ROLE PLAYED BY GLASS BOTTLES

One of the most notable discoveries to come from the bright British minds of the time, important not just for cider but for the wider world of drinks, was something that brings great pleasure to many today. At times a sign of excess and celebration, but now also as simple as the water we might buy, it was a discovery of something that led to many of the sparkling drinks we have today. Many might wrongly assume Champagne to be the oldest of sparkling wines, perhaps even the oldest of sparkling drinks, being one of the most venerated. But to explain cider's role in the story of sparkling drinks we must first delve a little into the history of Champagne, and strip back a few fallacies.

The first mention of sparkling "Champaign" was supposedly made in Sir George Ethridge's play *Man of Mode*, in 1676, but before the 18th century if wine made in the Champagne region of France had bubbles in it, it was both unintentional and considered a fault. In his wonderful book *Bursting Bubbles*, Robert Walters charts the truth of Champagne's rise and dispels many of the myths that have built up around it. Prime among them is the myth that Dom Pérignon invented Champagne—he did not. In fact there is no evidence to support Dom Pérignon having ever made even a single bottle of sparkling wine, and in all likelihood he went to great effort to ensure his wines did not sparkle, such was the reputation of the wines of the Abbey Saint-Pierre d'Hautvillers, and such was the dislike for sparkling wine by wine-makers in the region at the time.

Despite there being a statue of Dom Pérignon in the courtyard at Möet, there are apparently no surviving drawings or paintings of him, so this lovable old monk sculpted with a bottle in his hand is but from the imagination of its artist. Add to that the curious fact that Dom Pérignon died in 1715, yet Möet was not founded until 1743, and the ingrained association of the two today seems slightly odd, to say the least. But anyone can see the value of such a mythology for marketing, for the very concept of Champagne as a whole; it has been said that Dom Pérignon was blind and uttered the immortal words "Come quickly, I am drinking the stars!", yet he was not blind, and those immortal words were first made mortal in an advert around a century after his death. The plot is thick...

↑ The statue of Dom Pérignon in the courtyard of Möet & Chandon.

The key question we need to ask is what it takes to make any form of drink sparkle? Not just Champagne. Today we are so accustomed to drinks that are sparkling that they hold little of the uniqueness they would have just a few hundred years ago. Sparkling water can occur in nature, under the correct geological conditions, but I've never heard of wine gushing forth from rock, naturally full of volcanic gas. So if Dom Pérignon is not the ultimate genesis of Champagne, let alone sparkling drinks, who is?

From the south of France apparently hails the oldest record of sparkling wine being deliberately made, close to the border with Spain and the Catalan cork forests, in 1531. The manner of making was the Ancestral Method; it was likely discovered by accident and is often now referred to as Pet Nat (see page 145). This is where no extra sugar is added to create a secondary fermentation; instead the drink is put in bottle before its first fermentation has finished. But the Champagne is not made in this way—it requires a secondary fermentation to be made to occur, and this must be in the bottle (plus a few other things). So unlike prosecco, where the secondary fermentation usually happens in a tank, for the Champagne Method (see page 148) the secondary fermentation that makes the bubbles must occur in the bottle.

So let's take a step back to first principles, to the bottle itself. As anyone who has opened a warm bottle of Champagne will know (and as the wire cage that holds its cork attests), the amount of pressure in a Champagne bottle is immense. In fact it can be over 70 psi (4.8 bar), roughly twice the pressure of a car tire. So the bottles need to be strong, very strong. As already alluded to, to find the origin of these bottles, and indeed the very first secondary fermentations in bottles, we have to cross the English Channel and look to the era that saw the birth of modern science, turning to a number of gentlemen, whose efforts, intrigue, and positions made this method possible. And it just so happens that they liked their cider.

In England, in the late 1500s, concern began to grow about the depletion of the nation's forests, and the resulting supply of wood used in industries requiring high heat, such as glass-making. Particular concern was raised regarding naval ship-building, the ships of the time requiring thousands of trees each. So King James I forbade the use of wood in glass-making, with charcoal predominantly being used at the time. Glass-making was a fairly small but growing industry back then; medieval making had occurred but expertise had begun arriving in Britain from the glass-making centers of Europe, such as Venice, giving new impetus to the industry. Sir Robert Mansell, an admiral to King James I, acquired the royal monopoly or patent for glass-making, and began making in the west of England, close to a source of coal, likely being mined in Wales. Mansell was something of an entrepreneur and had acquired the monopoly, aware of the current fashion for imported Italian glass in England. At the time, the predominant demand produced glass that was fragile and brittle. A change from the use of charcoal to coal to power the furnaces yielded far higher heats, and this combined with certain impurities, in particular iron and manganese, that were likely derived from the coal, produced a far stronger glass. It became known as *verre anglais* by the French, being green in color, and apparently to this day such green bottle glass is often still called English Glass by wine-makers in Germany.

From here, the fascinating character Sir Kenelm Digby got involved; he was said to be a polymath, a diplomat, a founder of the Royal Society, a privateer, an alchemist, and a philosopher, and his father was even partially involved in the Gunpowder Plot to blow up Parliament in 1605. The strength of the bottles improved further under Digby's experimentation, and when he combined his efforts with a gentleman named James Howell, the manager of Mansell's Glassworks on Broad Street in London, a larger scale of production became possible. They made changes to the furnace design to feed more oxygen into the fire and heat it further still. Digby, working under license from Mansell, then set up a furnace close to the Forest of Dean, in the west of the county of Gloucestershire, very much in the realms of cider country. The shape of the bottles was not the same as the bottles we know today, with the bottles of the day more bulbous and with a huge indent (called a punt) in the base extending up into the bottle, for added strength.

Digby is also said to have been an early pioneer of using cork to seal a bottle. At the time there were good trading relations between England and Portugal, which produces more cork than any other nation on Earth. The lip created at the neck of a bottle at the time would have been used to tie the cork closed with string, being known as a string lip; string has, of course, since been replaced by wire, with this lip giving an edge for the wire cage to tighten against to hold the cork in place.

In 1642 the English Civil War began, and Digby was imprisoned for being a Royalist. Mansell's monopoly on glass-making came to an end, also because he was a Royalist and given that the monopoly was by royal warrant. Yet with glass now in existence that was strong enough to take the pressure, the world was but waiting for the rise of drinks that did sparkle abundantly. The invention of such strong bottles was pivotal, near necessary, for all sparkling drinks, not just those made with the method that has become known as the Champagne Method. Today glass is far purer and bottles are designed to greater strength from less glass, but the next time you hold an empty Champagne bottle in your hands, note its weight and think back to its origins. It is still true today that if the glass is weak, or the pressure of the sparkling drink inside the bottle too high, the bottle may explode.

Why go into such detail on the history of the Champagne Method and the discovery of the bottles that it requires? Well, think of the era and region in which much of this discovery occurred. It was in Britain, it very much

overlapped the key cider-making regions of Britain's heyday of fine cider-making, and many of the individuals involved were also cider-makers.

In the first reference to this, published in 1653, Ralph Austen notes that cider stored in bottles in this way "keeps a good many years." Then in 1662, on December 10th, a gentleman from Herefordshire named John Beale presented a paper to the Royal Society describing the addition of "a walnut of sugar" to a bottled cider to make it sparkle. It was known as a "Pot-gun drink," on account of it gushing from the bottle if it became too sparkling, being said

← Cider bottles made in the "Champagne Method."

→ Checking cider made with the same method as Champagne.

to fly about the room. The following year further papers were presented by cider-makers, including one that described the correct addition of leftover yeast to add upon bottling. So here we have the addition of both the sugar and yeast that is today known as the liqueur de tirage in sparkling wine-making. So the first Traditional Method sparkling wine was likely made in England, and was also quite possibly cider, not wine (although it is recorded that wine coopers of the time would also make sparkling wines in this manner).

At the turn of the 17th century such a method or bottle was being described in France as "English fashion," and by the 1720s the trade in bottled cider from Herefordshire into London was growing strong, with Daniel Defoe in the 1720s visiting Herefordshire and writing that:

*"We could get no beer or ale in their public houses, only cyder; and that so very good, so fine and so cheap, that we never found fault with the exchange; great quantities of this cyder are sent to London, even by land carriage, though*

*so remote, which is an evidence for the goodness of it, beyond contradiction."*

While most cider of the time came as draft from a barrel, the bottle helped lower the risk of the cider coming into contact with bacteria that would turn it to vinegar. Particularly when sparkling, the carbon dioxide gas that had been produced in the bottle filled the part of the bottle that did not contain cider, blocking oxygen from getting in and preserving the cider it was entombed with.

Digby, in his 1669 cookery book *The Closet of the Eminently Learned Sir Kenelme Digbie Knight Opened*, also describes technical advances in cider-making such as controlling the temperature of bottles by placing them in sand to keep them cool and stop them exploding in hot weather, and insulating them in hay in winter to stop them freezing. And Lord Scudamore was known to have "rare contrived cellars in his park for keeping cider with spring water running onto them," for just such a purpose. Wells were also used, with bottles hung in them or in small vaults down the shaft.

And in John Worlidge's *Vitum Brittanicum* of 1676, he describes a method of upending bottles, such that the spent yeast in the bottle would collect in the bottle neck, and could be removed with the first glass, and he even describes special racks to hold the bottles at an angle, that would be similar to the pupitres that are traditionally used in Champagne. This is still done today, with the collected yeast removed and the bottle resealed before sale, and is why Champagne has no sediment in it. It is often touted as a key part of the Champagne Method.

These details vary slightly depending on which writer you read; some individuals are made to seem more prominent than others, and as ever the murky world of history is clouded by distance and its capturing. But while there is no single definitive inventor of this bottle glass, and its evolution happened across around half a century, where it was invented seems clear. It was a technical discovery that opened the door to a whole new realm of pleasurable possibilities.

I should also note that I have heard of written evidence from Germany about such a method that predates the first references in England. So there may be more of this story to unearth!

← Bottles of amber cider.

## ORCHARD TRADITIONS

Back solely to cider. In the 17th century many new orchards were planted in Britain, and it was said that the acreage of orchard in some parts of England's West Country doubled. So-called "common cider" was made at this time by rehydrating pressed apple pomace with water, and then pressing it again. Also known as *small cider* or *ciderkin*, it was low in alcohol as a result, a lot like "small beer" (low-alcohol beer). It would have been more of a daily drink, lower in cost, and drunk prevalently across the countryside, even by children, with the finest ciders being the preserve of the better off. By the 18th century nearly all farms in Herefordshire had orchards of cider apples and perry pears; as farm laborers were often paid in cider and as much of the work was seasonal, such as during harvest time, the better your cider, the easier it would have been to get better laborers for your farm.

A custom came into full force across these centuries, that of wassailing. On the eve of Twelfth Night, the last of the 12 days of Christmas, on either January 5th or 6th, locals would gather in their orchards to enact the tradition in hope of a bountiful apple harvest the following season. Flaming torches usually lit the way as a procession headed into the orchard, to pour cider at the roots of an apple tree, and hang toast or cake from its branches, intended for the birds, robins, and blue tits especially; presumably this holds a slight practical purpose, giving them something to eat and so encouraging birds into the orchard that will help eat pests. And in Devon it's recorded the custom was to put a small boy into the branches, to play the role of "Tom Tit," crying out "Tit, Tit, more to eat." Often the biggest apple tree was chosen, a chant chanted, and then noise made by horns or the firing of shotguns, to scare away evil spirits.

It was apparently the final party of the Christmas holiday, and a good excuse to drink cider before returning to work. Many wassails happen today in cider regions across Britain, and around the world, in a revival of the custom. It all has rather a pagan feel to it, and is often accompanied by plentiful mulled cider. The sight of 50 to 100 flaming torches proceeding into an orchard is a rich and somewhat primal spectacle. For the sake of insurance I won't name any names, but I've seen the sight and heard the sound of shotguns sporadically firing, off in the distance, from different sides around a wassail, a conocled burst of flame, and a low booming, scaring away the evil spirits. The spirits notwithstanding, the shotguns would certainly make me think twice about trying to steal any apples from that orchard…

↑ An illustration from 1913 depicting the wassailing of an apple tree.

# THE RISE OF THE BIG BRANDS

Back in Britain, a new resurgence of better-quality cider had begun, taking note of the developments and refinements that had occured in wine across Europe in the past century or so. This era saw the founding of many of the big British cider-makers known today, such as Bulmers and Westons. Unlike France, Britain lacks such proud restrictions by law as to what can be called cider, and this has defined the mass market of cider we know today: a sweetened and carbonated drink poured by the pint, made in an industrial manner by the chemist's hand and knowledge. Think of this cider as factory-farmed, and factory-made.

Bulmers, the biggest cider-maker today, is now enormous and is owned by Heineken International. But in its early days it was a different thing. It was started in Herefordshire in 1887 by Percy Bulmer. Percy had suffered from bad asthma growing up, so bad in fact that he was not expected to reach adulthood and as such was not sent to school. When the surprise came that he had in fact grown up, he was left with little education and the question of what to do with his life. His mother advised something to do with eating and drinking, as they never went out of fashion, and his father's interest in local apples and pears also helped light the way. Over the following year or so his brother, Fred, who had gone to study at King's College Cambridge, had a job offer to be the tutor to the children of the King of Siam, but he turned it down to go make cider with Percy.

Their business grew, and around half a decade later Percy decided to go off to France, to learn more of the science side of things from its wine-makers. He made contact with some Champagne makers, and they showed him how Champagne was made. He returned full of knowledge and with literature on wine- and cider-making, and the Bulmers set about making cider by the same process as Champagne.

Originally called "Cider De Lux," then renamed "Pomagne," these "Champagne ciders" were made by Bulmers using the Champagne Method until around the 1950s. Their previous production site on Ryelands Street in Hereford is today the Hereford Cider Museum, and has the old "Champagne cider" cellars in its the basement—you can walk through them for yourself; they had capacity for thousands of bottles, each laid down to mature for perhaps a year and a half. Upstairs they have a private archive of bottles of such ciders, among which I found one that came from over a century ago. Other makers of the era also created "Champagne Ciders," such as Ridlers Champagne Cider, Daniel Phelps and Son Champagne Cider, and Whiteway's Champagne de Pomme. Some exquisite advertising posters were created to sell them, with gorgeous drawn and painted artworks.

Then came the 1960s and 70s, when the legal definition of cider in the UK, for duty purposes (currently defined by Excise notice 162), was put in place that still exists today: stating that cider need only be made from 35 percent apple juice, this "juice" can be from concentrate, and the rest could be water, plus a list of other permissible things. It left a lot of room open for mass-market cider to dumb down what it made, and like a self-fulfilling prophecy, this room for maneuver has been filled further and further ever since. Often today a "cider" may be made by fermenting concentrate up to high alcohols, perhaps 10 or 12 percent or so, and then this is cut back with water to get to the desired 4.2–4.5% abv. As noted, in France it has to be 100 percent juice, although apparently concentrate can be used, and in the USA the level is 50 percent.

Excise duty had not been applied to cider in Britain for the 50 years prior to this duty being levied, and so all of a sudden cider faced new costs; either prices had to rise, or the cider itself had to be made more cheaply. The prevailing model for large cider-makers became one based on the brewing industry, rather than the world of wine. The same era, up until the late 1980s, saw lots of buyouts and mergers, by Bulmers in particular. Big makers increased their size by buying up the many medium-size makers, a process that has resulted in the main half a dozen or so "cider" brands we know in Britain today.

Then, in 2006, Magners was rolled out across the UK, and the Magners boom took off. Poured over a glass full of ice, having been launched in a very hot summer, it took off like wildfire and saw a new generation of drinkers warming to cider. Rather than a draft product poured from a tap, it came in bottles, and the ice in the glass meant that you could not pour a whole bottle out in one go, so customers had to take the bottle with them from the bar. The result was pubs everywhere with Magners bottles, advertising themselves on tables.

# CIDER TODAY

In the past decade or so "cider" in Britain has shifted somewhat again, further fulfilling its mass-market prophecy, with so called "fruit ciders." They contain the flavors of fruits other than the apple, often tropical ones. And so "cider" in Britain finds itself in a tricky situation, through seeds largely self-sown, made in the manner of brewing, and with an audience led a world away from all that cider can be at its best, fullest form.

In my view, the true failing of what "cider" has become in the mass market today is that the greatest percentage volume of it is but a shadow of what it could be. I think everything has its place—except a few things which seem to me to be on the predatory "white cider" (super-strength, very cheap cider, which has no color) end of the spectrum. I don't dislike a cold and easy cider every now and then, and do not wish the best ciders to reach the ridiculous prices that wine often can, but I feel we, the public, are missing a whole world of wonderment, that is held at bay by the industrial norms of the cider world today. We can have things so much better, more in all manners: more variety, more quality, more provenance, and more flavor.

I find it somewhat nuts, knowing all this, how much a bottle or pint of such concentrate "cider" can cost in a pub—in London it can be over £5. Many mass-market ciders strike me as a rip-off, knowing a little of how they are made, when compared to the finest ciders I know. The finest may be more expensive per milliliter, but strike me as better value when you know the difference in taste, and also in their making. The finest ciders are, however, little known, and so I often hear the statement "That's expensive for a cider," so I explain that it is made with the full Champagne Method (see page 148), and point out that despite this even one of the best Champagne ciders on the planet will cost less than even a mediocre Champagne. As things are mostly seen before they are tasted, especially prices, a convert is then made when the cider is actually tasted, the quality speaking for itself. It also seems surreal to me, that in Britain mass-market ciders pay the same duty on their products as the best small-batch cider-makers, and yet how they are made is so very different. It is largely a failing of our lawmakers, that the standards they set allow things to be as they are.

→ Fine cider goes wonderfully well with food, and is drunk like wine.

"Moral hazard" is a term often used in economics, to describe a situation where one party takes a risk knowing that another party will bear the cost if that risk leads to negative consequences. If the consequences of an action are not borne by the actor taking that risk, it's a very dangerous precedent, particularly for regulators, to allow in a market. An asymmetry of information —with one party knowing more about its intentions than another—is often a cause of moral hazard; where the risk-taker might even have an incentive, such as profit, to act inappropriately from the perspective of the person paying the bill if it goes wrong.

I see the loose cider legislation in Britain as a moral hazard for the public: if you view the role of the government as acting on behalf of the people, and you include the quality of food and drink within this mantle, the introduction of this legislation set the stage for things to get as industrialized as they have. The consequences that resulted are being borne by us the public, in the quality of the cider we have to drink. The public awareness and knowledge of the quality cider can have has been so eroded over the past half century that this loose legislation was like a frog in water slowly being brought to the boil. A gradual erosion can go unnoticed, especially if the thing itself is already far from its former glory, the memory lost.

# FRUIT CONCENTRATE AND FRUIT CIDERS

A similar effect exists in my view, a moral hazard of inevitability, for "cider" makers who use concentrate: if you are willing to take that step, to increase efficiency and profitability, at the potential expense of the customer, and the quality of their drink, you are not incentivized to maintain or improve the quality of what you were already making. Quality becomes compromised for other factors, which lead the incentive structure. This risk is allowed by legislation, and the two are fatally intertwined.

But the possible consequences of using concentrate seem wide-reaching: if you have stores of concentrate which act as an insurance policy against a bad season, why work seasonally at all? Why work with fresh juice at all? Why even stay true to the original form of the thing at all, cider, made from apples; why not add berry concentrate, etc? Some would say it is the only way to make cider and to innovate on this scale, but that in itself is a sad state of affairs, and the wine world would suggest otherwise, where more makers of a smaller scale can make a greater volume than one or two goliaths, and all of a greater quality.

So in many ways it's a somewhat logical step for the mass-market cider-maker, following the use of as little as 35 percent apple juice concentrate, to move to using concentrate and flavors from fruits other than apples. The irony is that these "fruit ciders" actually fetch a far higher duty than most cider, technically being classed as made wines, going too far even for the legislation. So this efficiency and innovation drive has actually taken "cider" to more expensive duty levels; guess which compromises results, higher prices for the customer? Or cost-cutting on the product itself?

Some might look to the past, to justify such "fruit ciders" as authentic, as centuries ago many things were added to cider and wine, such as ginger, herbs, spices. But back then this was usually done to remedy a thing gone bad, such was the short lifespan of a drink at its prime before science really understood how to make it last longer. And I doubt there were passionfruit or kiwi ciders about in the Middle Ages; such "ciders" today are simply a means of going beyond the apple, having squeezed it beyond its nature.

But what's so bad about using concentrate? Well, ignoring the difference most of us know in taste between fresh pressed apple, orange, or other such fruit juices, and their counterparts made from concentrate and bought from the supermarket, the nature of creating and using concentrate is profound, as the level of processing it puts the apple juice through is extreme. The vast majority of the apple juice's flavor and aroma are lost in the concentration process. The aroma that is lost in evaporation can supposedly be captured, and may then be reintroduced, or in other cases sold off as an "essence of apple" flavoring. But then you are chasing the tail of something superior, the original juice complete with natural aroma, and merely trying to simulate it.

It's known in the world of fine cheese that such invasive processes (pasteurization and micro-filtration, for example) disrupt the connection between milk and cheese flavor. And in this comparison, these cheese-makers aren't even making concentrate from their raw material; that would be a far more invasive process. But in both cider- and cheese-making such processes are often done in pre-production, and the effect of them leans toward a flattening of the results, to something more proximal. You lose the virtues of variety and a more natural complexity.

It is hard to know how many of the biggest "cider" makers make their cider, as they typically don't like to release information about their processes. But some overly eager marketing person at a big cider-maker will now be keen to point out that concentrate comes (originally) from apples, and those apples come from a season. And some would also argue that the ciders of the mass market can be considered the "highest quality," as they display the fullest extent of scientific control and intentionality. To me that's like arguing that nothing is artificial because everything ultimately came from the Universe... Gradation exists, and artificiality is a scale that gets more extreme the more man intervenes in the making of something. The key factors to look at in any gauging of how natural something is are how far it has come from its most raw form, and the intention behind an action being applied to it. The key intention behind using concentrate in cider-making is to remove seasonality from the process, in order to save space and improve efficiency.

And personally, I have never tasted anything made in large or small volumes with the greatest prominence on the chemistry, that even comes close to the virtues and sheer depth of taste that a wild yeast-fermented cider can achieve. Surely the scientist should be the first to admit the sheer complexity and multitude of factors that affect the fermentation of cider, and surely they should be the most knowing of all the elements naturally underway when fresh apple juice is fermented by wild yeasts (see page 128).

# THE CHALLENGES FOR TODAY'S CIDER-MAKERS

I think that some smaller cider-makers today become entirely beholden to the science, seeing it alone as the intention, following a path set by the large mass-market makers, but with none of their wider set-up. And so they are competing with huge businesses, paying the same duty levels, but bewitched by the path set by these large-scale makers, with science in their eyes. Their small scale may well allow them to make cider that is better, but how much so will be limited, always beholden to these industrial ideals.

One key thing to know about the finest makers, those favoring wild yeasts, full juice, and minimal intervention in the fermentation itself, is that they know the science. They need to, to create the finest ciders while working in the manner they do. As they are not taking the chemists' approach of intervening, they have fewer tools to work with, and the choices they make from the very start set the pieces on the board upon which the wild yeasts play. But the key thing that differentiates these makers is that they are not blinded by the science; instead they utilize it to further their wider intentions, the greatest of which is taste. They don't let the objective facts of science, fascinating though they are, become mistaken for quality in their own right.

I agree with their intentions; I want more: more taste, more depth, more variety, and more complexity. And I do not want things to be reduced to some homogeneous ideal, simply because it's the most efficient to make, or scored highest in the market research (which only tends to look for a single answer, and rarely questions the very foundations upon which it occurs, whether intentionally or otherwise).

The difficulties for small, fine cider-makers today in competing with the big "cider" makers for the identity of what cider is, is that most members of the public do not know or have not tasted the difference, instead thinking of cider as just one thing. It is a question of quality over quantity, but not all of the cards are on the table. It's not a straight choice between the mass-market ciders and the fine ciders that are emerging. People do not know what they are missing; to paraphrase Henry Ford on the arrival of the automobile: "If I had asked people what they wanted, they would have said a faster horse."

The best makers push up against this reality in order to improve it. That's their burden, as much as simply questions of quality are, as is the understanding the wider world needs to gain of cider they must convey.

So the kind of cider I am speaking about in the coming chapters, and throughout this book, is not the mass-market kind of cider; it is not the industrial product found in pubs and supermarkets across the land. When I speak about the season of cider-making, you have to remember that the mass market barely has a season; they use concentrate precisely so they can defy the season and spread out when they begin a fermentation. Instead, in the coming chapters, we will get some insight and set some definition in the world of the New Wave of fine cider-makers, who are setting the benchmark for the future of cider.

And this new wave is not just emerging as a new force in old and long established cider regions, but almost independently in all sorts of regions; communities of like-minded makers, establishing the reputation of an emerging region, such as in Scotland, or in the Baltic States (as the Baltic Cider Awards attest). Each along its own path, doing things in its own pioneering way.

→ Small-batch cider-makers face the challenge of making the general public aware of the superior quality of their ciders.

CHAPTER 3

# Apples for Cider-making

In 2018, in the USA just three apple varieties made up over 50 percent of the apples sold: the Honeycrisp, the Gala, and the Fuji. Over 80 percent of the apples sold were from just nine varieties. Of course these were apples bred and sold for eating, not cooking or cider-making, but given all that we now know of the genetic diversity inherent in the reproduction of apples (see page 22), it highlights a surreal point: how much we seem to sacrifice variety for an easy abundance of one or two favored forms in our food and drink supply chain.

A big question to ask about apple varieties, with the intention of using them to make cider, is which are best to use? The answer would seem obvious, those that make the cider that tastes best, but as we already know from the use of concentrate (see pages 56–57), this is not the only version of the "fittest" at play. Take the three eating apples just mentioned—these are apples for which "the fittest" means fittest for industrial production and profitability, and these factors vie with taste to define what triumphs. Their disease resistance, their abundant cropping, and their aesthetic appearance are all factors that affect the profit that can be derived from their growing. These are all important considerations, and a business needs to make money to survive, but if the balance isn't right, taste isn't necessarily incentivized to be the primary aim. And this is clearly evident in the use of as little as 35-percent apple concentrate in mass-market cider-making in Britain.

# VARIETY VS VOLUME

Variety is also a thing that often seems diminished under such a system of food and drink production. Even from what little I know of it, this raises some interesting questions: Do our massive-scale methods of making give such a leg up to a chosen few ingredients and products, that we lose much of the wider "gene pool" from which to choose? And are we losing some complexity of choice both in terms of naturally occurring ingredients and the final products made from them? Is it complexity that forms the basis of things being improved, and refined? And can the successes and advances of our current system of food and drink production be harnessed to favor products of greater provenance and locality?

This might sound like a question of past vs present, but I am wary of the ease with which the past can simply be fetishized and misinterpreted, and I'm not simply referring to the past. This limiting of variety would certainly seem true of the few eating apples just mentioned, giving us—the customer—so few options to choose between. And the same is true of mass-market cider, where a few near indistinguishable options reign supreme, with little variety to be found and an apparent sapping of quality having occurred over past decades.

I also think here of other experiences that seem increasingly homogenized, such as those coffee-shop chains that dominate; enormous lattes, more abundant than flavorful, being drunk in different parts of the world but in the exact same surroundings. It seems so often today that an established ideal or product triumphs through industrial means, losing many of its ideals in the process, and becoming but a shadow of the original form. I think also of the pub-chain menu, the supermarket shelves, and the fast-food giants. For sure, such systems of food and drink have bought us an abundance of what were before lesser known things, but the question is getting louder in the ether: what has been lost due to the speed and structure of this system?

Today, the players in the world that create our food and drink, each in their own struggle to survive, often seem to lean toward one equation of profitability, one genetic profile if you will. Be it reliant on low-cost labor farming halfway around the world, or simply the same thing done millions upon millions of times over with meticulous control. How often does this lead to optimization of the systems of production, over optimization of the output? There are, of course, enclaves of difference, rebellion, and simply those who have survived the shift, but the thing I am most interested in, and see clearly being questioned in the world of cider, is what has been lost in this process?

My thoughts of course come merely from my own perspective, and certainly the resources of such a system as we currently have can be turned to incredible things. In Britain for example, at the East Malling Research Station in Kent, researchers apparently plant some 20,000 apple seeds each year, all from apples that were pollinated by hand. Think of all the varieties that result, all with countless little genetic variations. But of course the ultimate intention of this is a commercial one—they are searching for the next apple that might join the small ranks of those on the supermarket shelves. Because across a span of some 20 or so years, as the chosen trees grow and fruit, they are tested for how fitting they are, to be eaten, to be grown at vast scales, and when the two decades are up, but a few possibles remain in the running and are commercially released. I do wonder, if only cider was on the minds of those researchers, not just the supermarkets' next aesthetic apple, the flavors that might exist and the ciders that might result...

But such an example also reflects just how much of an impact we humans now have on the workings of things previously done by nature, especially where genetic diversity is concerned. We all know an element of this truth, from all of the dog breeds we own to the livestock in the fields—of all the mammals on

→ Herefordshire has many huge orchards, such as this one in blossom.

Earth, 36 percent are now humans, 60 percent are our livestock, and just 4 percent are wild mammals. But the fullest industrial reach of this in the food and drink industries is perhaps a little less known.

For example, the wonderful book *Reinventing the Wheel*, by Bronwen and Francis Percival, highlights this in the world of cattle farming: the dominant variety of dairy cow across the world is the Holstein Friesian. Of the 30 or so million Holsteins in the world, such is the manipulation by artificial insemination and selective breeding, mostly only since the 1950s, that in North America all of the Holstein bull semen available for artificial insemination is apparently descended from just two bulls. A single bull is estimated to have fathered some 500,000 offspring, by virtue of artificial insemination. And a bull called Pawnee Farm Arlinda Chief that was only born in 1962 is the source of genes for some 14 percent of the entire US dairy herd today. Chosen of course for certain traits, he nonetheless is not perfect, being a carrier of a genetic defect that causes miscarriages in some offspring. This defect alone has caused genetic defects to an economic impact to the industry estimated at around $400 million. But the estimated value from this bull's superior milk production genetics sit at $25 billion. One of these numbers is of course far fitter than the other.

What do we gain and what do we sacrifice for this ability to select so specifically how the raw ingredients for our food and drink will be? My mind first leaps to the question of do we lose the diversity, the variety, from which we will be able to choose in the future? Are we speeding along the evolution of these animals, or pulling it off down a side road that may turn out to be a dead end? And by such a system of production do we get something "better," faster, and cheaper, but in doing so erode the very basis from which it came to prominence, that of variety? And of course who does this favor—we the customer, or the industrial producer? Like trading the supermarket readymeal for the local butcher...

Interestingly, to make what might seem like an obscure comparison, even in the cutting-edge world of artificial intelligence and machine learning, it is widely acknowledged that diversity is key to creating successful genetic algorithms

← Apples can be the most wonderfully varied things.

↑ The National Perry Pear Collection, in Gloucestershire, is home to over 100 different varieties of perry pear.

(where iterative concepts from evolutionary biology are applied to digitized problem solving). Such evolution would seem to rely on a competition of many, and a refinement to too few contenders would seem to lessen the quality of the overall outcome.

For me, where cider is concerned, the natural variety and complexity of apple varieties are a source of charming fascination. For what makes for a better world to explore than one of relished abundance and ever-present possibility, the intrigue of the new, and the uncertain? When everything you taste is slightly different, you are not limited to the predictability of a homogenized, seasonless cider, one that will never change, save when a focus group says it should. Yes, there can be lows in variety, as is the reality of life as a whole, but so too can there be soaring highs, and what is a pleasure with nothing to contrast it to? Where apple and pear varieties are concerned, there are those wonderful champions who know this, and do what they can to keep the variety alive: like Tom Oliver, rediscovering the Coppy perry pear, or the wonderful National Perry Pear Collection, at Hartpury in Gloucestershire, which, with the wonderful work of Jim Chapman, has over 100 different varieties of perry pear growing in its orchards.

It is variety that makes for some of the greatest joy that fine cider can provide: the differences between each apple variety, region, season, and maker. There is so much to explore, both in the variety of apples from which it is made and the beautiful spectrum of ciders that result.

# FRUIT IDENTIFICATION

I wouldn't be able to tell you about all the apples used to make cider or the pears used to make perry, and no one could; it's not simply that so many varieties exist in the world, but that they can also be very localized. Perhaps one of the best examples of this comes from Find & Foster (see page 152), made by Polly and Mat Hilton in Devon. Their apples come from trees spread far and wide. A couple of years ago, after discovering that Devon has lost 90 percent of its orchards since World War 2, Polly got a conservation map and went searching to see which orchards listed on the map remained. She found 25 within a 5-mile radius of her house; many lost until her rediscovery, and sometimes just a few ancient trees left in the corner of a field. Many were unloved and overrun, dense and thick with mistletoe, unpruned for decades, and falling over under their own weight. They now maintain these orchards and drive the back lanes of Devon with their Italian mountain tractor, mowing the long grass under the apple trees, often on steep hillsides, in dense Devon valleys that sit not far from the sea.

Working with the most technically complex methods, and the astuteness to pull them off, one of Polly and Mat's most complex bottles is their Methode Traditionelle, made using the Champagne Method (see page 148). Last season's had some 27 apple varieties in its blend, most of them unknown or unidentified. Some they know, including local characters like the Cornish Longstem apple, which holds a fascinating acidity and lime-green skin. It picks late and so can sit on the tree once the leaves have gone, looking like baubles. They keep photographs and records, but most of the apples they work with for this blend they know only by taste and experience. It's a manner of making which is highly reliant on instinct and a near-perfect palate; even blending by taste from the raw juices, knowing what will change in the taste as the fermentation does its thing.

In Herefordshire there are far better networks for identifying apple and pear varieties, with organizations like the Marcher Apple Network—a great reflection of the wisdom of age. At events in Herefordshire where identification is offered to visitors bringing fruit with them, wise elders are sat behind a table and plied with plentiful cups of tea. They look closely at apples, turning them in their hands and discussing gently what variety they think it might be, like contestants on a panel show conferring among themselves, but with less rush.

It's a fascinating skill to have, the sheer experience to differentiate between such subtle variations in characteristics. It's a process of elimination, going through stages of recognition, every little detail from the color and texture

→ James Marsden picking perry pears at Gregg's Pit in Herefordshire.

of the skin, to the size and form of the apple; and yet you always have to remember that even if all of the apples that grow on the tree are the same variety, each will still vary in size, ripeness (skin color, etc. can change with ripeness), and other markings, like its blush. So none is likely to be an archetypal reflection of the specific variety that it nonetheless is.

Now, of course, an archive of varieties, logged by DNA, is being built so such wisdom can live on, in scientific precision. But there'll always be the charms of the outliers, the varieties that no one knows, and new ones emerging all of the time.

# CIDER APPLES

When you think of the apples we most commonly find, i.e. those massive few found in the supermarkets and grocery stores across the globe, tastes and textures are surely conjured to mind. But these eating apples are rather different from the realm of historic cider apples of Britain. They might have some family resemblances, in shape or in color, but their taste is usually a very different thing as they were not chosen for orcharding based on their taste when eaten, but their taste when made into cider.

So what are cider apples? Put simply, they are apples that have been commonly used for cider-making. They have been chosen and used across the past few centuries by cider-makers for the properties they have and the propensity of these properties to make good cider. Good is, of course, a subjective term but there are a few objective characteristics that cider apples tend to hold: high sugar levels and a relatively high tannin content.

Tannins are a key part of many cider apples, but what are tannins? They are mostly a textural sensation, and you will recognize the experience of them from tea and red wine. They are technically a class of polyphenols, which bind with proteins in your saliva, supposedly increasing the viscosity of your saliva and the friction in your mouth. They impart an astringent, bitter sensation. Your teeth can feel rough, with a certain furriness, and you can feel a drying sensation in the mouth. So perhaps the simplest way to think of tannins is as texture and bitterness; they contribute a lot to what I would call the body of a cider.

→ The choice of which apple to use in a cider can make a huge difference.

The tannins in apples supposedly exist in the flesh, not just the skin, unlike wine grapes where the tannins concentrate on the skins. But, in spite of them being a key component in many of the best ciders and wines, their existence in plants in nature is supposedly as a bitter deterrent to animals, to stop the plant being eaten. With leaves, such as tea leaves, this makes a lot of sense, as if the leaves are eaten they are simply lost from the plant. But for the fruit of the plant, such as apples and grapes, this is a little less logical to me, as the seeds they contain need to be transported and much of the properties of their existence, such as beautiful blossom and sweet sugary taste, is specifically adapted to attract animals to them, to pollinate and propagate this fruit. But nonetheless tannins are there in apples, and can create some exquisite results in cider.

In cider, tannins have natural preservative and antioxidant properties. They react with oxygen, and this has a pronounced effect on the appearance of a cider. It's the same principle as cutting open an apple and leaving it for a few minutes. What does it do? The exposed flesh of the apple turns brown. This is caused by an enzyme reacting with oxygen and the tannins, creating a brown pigment. This simple color change gives us a great little rule of thumb: the darker in tone (the more amber to umber) a cider, the more tannic it is likely to be. This is simply because if there are more tannins in the cider, there are more tannins that can oxidize and brown. But also because less tannic ciders tend to come from more acidic apples. It is not always the only factor, such darker colors can come from such things as barrel aging or excessive oxygen contact, for example. But as a general rule, it provides a great tool. Learn how you feel about tannins, and you'll get to know your color chart.

Cider apples can be divided into four categories called sharps, bittersharps, sweets, and bittersweets—effectively variations based on acidity and tannin content. This classification was created at the Long Ashton Research Station near Bristol, which was founded a little over a century ago, and shut down just after the millennium. A blended cider will often use a mix of varieties from these different categories, in order to give balance and complexity to the cider.

It has taken a considerable amount of time and intent for the array of cider apple varieties we have today, such as those we see in England and France, to become established. And while the bulk of fine cider made today will be produced with these apples, I am not wedded to the idea that only they can be used. In my view, the quality of a cider can be judged on its own merits. Tastes vary, particularly over time, and tradition can be limiting as well as rewarding. The key is how the apple variety is used, and if the cider is made in a manner that makes the most of that specific variety.

Of course the properties of these traditional cider apples give some undeniable advantages, like the complexities yielded from higher alcohols and a greater depth of fermentation, or the complexity of tannins. Eating and dessert apples can be harder to coax depth and complexity from, but I do not believe that all you might want a cider to be is limited to these traditional cider apple varieties. There is no single ideal set of characteristics, and why should things have to stick solely to historical favorings, when new possibilities can reap wonderful rewards?

This question of the "fitness" of an apple for cider-making is an interesting one, and its answer is being slightly reshaped by the New Wave of cider-makers, particularly those working in the USA. As a result, a new chapter of possibility has been opened up using non-traditional cider apples. So what are these varieties if not cider apples? As hinted at, they are on the eating and dessert end of the apple spectrum. The cider they produce will tend to be lower in tannin, with their acidity more prominent on the palate. I think of them like the white wine of the cider world, compared to the red wine—with its tannins and often higher alcohol—of the tannic, robust traditional cider apples.

In Britain there is a rough divide between the west and the east of the country as to where traditional and non-traditional cider apples are mostly grown, and thus the types of cider made within these regions. The West Country (the southwest) of England is the heartland of traditional cider apples, often making tannic, full-bodied ciders, whereas the southeast predominantly grows eating and dessert apples, often making lighter, more acidity-orientated ciders. Therefore I often speak of the distinction between these kinds of apples as "East Coast" fruit and "West Coast" fruit.

But another way you could divide it, one that is a little more global, and is based more on the properties of the cider that results from these different categories of apples, takes reference from the world of wine: Old World cider and New World cider. The Old World is marked by tradition, specifically the traditional cider apple varieties it is accustomed to, and its ciders, like its

↑ West Coast fruit.

apples, have been refined over centuries in accordance with certain ideals. But in the New World, as the New Wave of cider-making has taken hold in Britain, the USA, and other parts of the world, the potential of eating and dessert apples to make fine ciders that are different to tradition has been well proven. As a result, New World cider and Old World cider are more styles (based on the apples used) than geographically specific designations of origin. But the same is of course true for these terms as used in wine: New World wine being more fruitful, often with more intense oak from the barrel, and Old World wine pertaining to properties traditionally sought after in the traditional wine-making regions of Europe. Neither, however, are limited to just one region and both can be made side by side.

# SOME COMMON CIDER APPLE VARIETIES

I don't know the apple varieties used for cider in the way a cider-maker might; I know them from the other end, that of the drinker. So how to go farther and give you an understanding of cider apples as a whole, as I know them? Perhaps the best way to think of cider apples overall is akin to wine grapes, where most people will know just a handful of key grape varieties, perhaps only their most or least favorite, or those that have come to dominate our shelves and wine lists. Knowing a few apples in this way gives you a means of choosing between ciders that are new to you, based on your liking of a specific variety, or others similar to it.

Here I am choosing a few apple varieties to turn a spotlight on. They are some of the more prominent varieties, and they will crop up a lot as you delve deeper into the new world of fine cider. They are varieties cider-makers often use in the UK and USA, but these few examples are also greater than the sum of their parts, suggestive of the vastness of possibility and the many corners of uniquenesses, across all apples.

Some varieties you get to know and recognize by taste alone after enough experience, with certain key characteristics always making themselves evident. And for the specific apple varieties we are going to focus on, I will note the predominant flavors each seems to display, from my experience of their taste.

One last thing to say about both apple and pear trees is that as they must be grafted (see pages 24–25), over time any viruses and infections that build up in a parent tree are passed along in the graft, and so the variety gets weaker and degrades, lowering in quality and productiveness. This usually gives a variety that lasts not much longer than a few centuries during which it will be at its peak. For example, research in the 1870s by the Woolhope Naturalists' Field Club of Hereford found that most of the best apple varieties mentioned in the literature of the previous two centuries had disappeared. The best apple varieties for cider-making were recorded in exquisite books, called Pomonas, which contained wonderful drawings of the apple varieties, along with descriptions. One of the most famous was the *Herefordshire Pomona* by Robert Hogg and Henry Bull from 1876; only some 600 were made and today a copy is said to cost over US$12,000 (£10,000). So the varieties available to make cider form part of an ever-changing spectrum.

Imagine the years a wonderful new apple or pear variety may exist, a single tree growing wild from a seed, before it was discovered and first tasted. How many seasons it may have seen, tucked away, ticking through the cycles of summer sun and winter rain. Then, upon its discovery, having to graft whole new trees from its buds, to wait years for those to reap fruit. Imagine this for the Yarlington Mill apple (see page 75), said to have been discovered at the end of the 19th century, growing from a wall by the mill in the village of Yarlington in Somerset. Not long over a century since this variety was discovered, a vast number of trees of that variety now exist across the world, all stemming back to that single tree, grafts upon grafts. The tale of Adam and Eve might purport to tell of one common ancestor for all of man, but for each apple variety there is indeed one common ancestor; no matter how abundant it might now be, any variety has an origin of one.

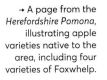

→ A page from the *Herefordshire Pomona*, illustrating apple varieties native to the area, including four varieties of Foxwhelp.

# TWO USA CIDER APPLES

## • NORTHERN SPY

For Ryan Burk of Angry Orchard Innovation Cider House, Walden, New York (see page 117), the Northern Spy apple has a personal significance because it's an apple that was discovered in New York State, close to where he grew up. Today, it's mostly grown in Michigan and New York State, and the variety is a couple of hundred years old.

Ryan picks it from the tree fairly late, so in November it has a lot of really fresh character. "It has a nice bracing acidity that's right to blend with Bittersweet varieties; it's a complimenter and a lifter of such varieties."

Ryan explains, "Often the apple isn't grown in other parts of the country as it really

↑ The Northern Spy.

needs time to develop on the tree, into the fall; it needs the cold winter. So to me it's very much an example of a good terroir-driven variety, because if you take it out of its native land, it's less likely to be as great as it actually is. If the Northern Spy's being grown along the southern shore of Lake Ontario, for example, you're going to have really mineral-driven acidity, and it's not going to taste the same when it's grown in other parts of the country."

## • MACINTOSH

Eleanor Léger of Eden Specialty Ciders, Vermont, New England (see page 114) describes this variety: "The Macintosh is a terroir apple in New England, it was discovered in Ontario across the border. It's a 19th-century apple and if you pick it and press it right around harvest, as opposed to out of cold storage after six months, it's got a tremendous acidity and wonderful aromatics, so it's a great component in blending."

↗ A cross-section of the Macintosh.

# THREE UK CIDER APPLES

## • YARLINGTON MILL

The Yarlington Mill is one of my favorite cider apples. It can work wonderfully as a single variety, or in a blend. With a medium level of tannin and relatively low level of acidity, ciders made from it have archetypal smoky and at times herbaceous or even slightly medicinal notes. Its home may be Somerset but it grows very well in Herefordshire, and also lends itself well to Keeving (see page 154). The apple itself has a conocled shape, and when mature holds bright, deep red and yellow markings.

## • DABINETT

The Dabinett is said to be the most prevalent cider apple grown in the UK. It is thought to have been found by a Mr William Dabinett growing as a wildling (growing naturally from a seed) at the start of the 20th century. The name "Dabinett" is historically considered a common surname in south Somerset, and the variety is said to have derived from a seed of the Chisel Jersey apple, another wonderful cider apple. Relatively low in acid and fairly high in tannin, its taste is marked by a unique savory, almost meaty taste, that can even be reminiscent of fennel salami when used as a single variety. It can make a fascinating single-variety cider, but is also commonly used in blends.

## • FOXWHELP

The Foxwhelp apple seems an interesting exception to the rule that a variety only lasts a few centuries; it is one of the oldest known cider apples still in use today, with its discovery being pre-1600s. There are, however, both an "Old" and a "Rejuvenated" Foxwhelp among others described in the *Herefordshire Pomona* (see preceding pages), suggesting that it is not as it once was. It's a very unique apple, and is sometime described as the "Riesling" of cider apples, given that it holds a very high acidity. With a fascinating rhubarb-like tartness and at times a strawberry aroma, it makes for a most useful variety when blending, and even a very small amount added to a blend can have a notable effect.

## PERRY: THE COMPATRIOT

The saying goes that the best perry is made in sight of May Hill. This hill, rising 970 ft (296m) above the surrounding Gloucestershire country, lies a little north of the Severn Estuary. The soft curve of this risen mass gives way to a wide flat top, from which you can look down across the waters of the River Severn to the south, as they become mercurial from the sun's glow. From here the River Severn flows into the Bristol Channel, and out to the sea to the south of Ireland, before reaching the expanse of the Atlantic Ocean.

It is a most distinctive hill, being monumental in scale and simplicity. Ponies roam along the paths that sit upon its waist, and all told it makes up some 75 acres (30 hectares) of common land, to be used by all for grazing, collecting firewood, etc. The first time I set out to see the view from atop

↓ May Hill.

this mohicaned mound, at sunrise one morning, these characterful ponies came speeding toward me. Worrying for a moment I was being charged, in a challenge from the gatekeepers of this hill, their pace was abated a few meters away and I could carry on to see the new day's sun cast its first gaze upon that which it had left alone all night.

May Hill is actually a good metaphor for perry pear trees and orchards as a whole, so distinctive and seemingly natural, yet altered by the hand of man. A phalanx of Corsican pines sit sentry upon its top, having been planted in 1887 to mark Queen Victoria's Golden Jubilee. In that morning's light their eastward sides were dusted with brass, and down by their trunks long shadows trailed westward. This block of trees form May Hill's unique profile, its mohawk, that makes it so exceptionally noticeable today from far away. The old saying of its role in the making of the best perry notwithstanding, it is a dominant feature and outline in the land, and it sits at the heart of what has been for centuries perhaps the greatest enclave of perry-making on the planet. Gloucestershire is abundant with wonderful old perry pear orchards, these noble giants of trees, as is Herefordshire, the border to which lies just a few hundred meters to the northwest of May Hill.

But what is perry? Often referred to (erroneously) as "pear cider," it is the juice of pears, the fruit sugars of which have been fermented to alcohol by yeasts. Just as with cider apples, there are certain varieties of pear, called perry pears, that have historically been selected and used for perry-making, owing to their desired properties. However, as perry is not a style of cider, it is not in reality "pear cider," and it could be with the greatest ease in the world a book by itself. It's a thing of finer charms, and of unique subtlety and rarity. I say it is not "pear cider" for two reasons: cider is made with apples, perry with pears, so pear cider does not make sense as a term. But also, while good cider and perry are made in hugely interrelated ways, "pear cider" and perry are not. Pear cider is almost irrevocably an industrial product, being mostly made from concentrate, yet perry is almost exclusively a small batch, hands-on thing, made from perry pears.

There are a number of reasons for this small-batch requisite. Firstly, pears rot from the inside out, and some can be ripe for a very short amount of time, meaning working with large volumes of them can be difficult. But also as the trees from which they come tend historically to be huge in scale, making the pears of the upper branches near inaccessible, and not conducive to the machine picking of the mass-market method. Where apples float, pears do not, so water cannot be used to move them around by their own buoyancy. And they can also be rather difficult to press; I remember being told of a special technique used by the wonderful perry-maker Jörg Geiger, who makes perry on the northern side of the Swabian Alps, near Stuttgart in Germany. Such can be the density of some of the pears they work with, such as the Champagner Bratbirner pear, that even with their powerful press the pears will not always actually press. Add to this the more acute skill required of the maker in fermenting perry, and you can understand a little of its uniqueness.

To frame the rest of this book with perry in mind, most of what you can do with cider, in terms of techniques and styles, you can do with perry. Often it is harder, such as in the case of *Keeving* (see page 154). But the main objective difference between perry pears and cider apples is that perry pears contain a sugar type called sorbitol that does not ferment, so perry tends to retain a higher level of natural sweetness than cider. This can give it a fascinating slight creaminess and an abundance of exquisite natural sweetness; think floral sweet, like the succulence of nectar in a flower that intoxicates you to smell it again and again.

Two perry pears—the Thorn and the Blakeney Red—exemplify some of the qualities perry can have. Perries made with the Thorn have an archetypal reminiscence of grapefruit, not the bitterness but the succulent fruity side with just a hint of tartness. The Thorn stands wonderfully alone when used as a single variety. The Blakeney Red, however, is a little less showy; it often forms a key part of a blend and has archetypal notes of elderflower. It is a rosy, more perfumed thing, with a nice bit of tannin to it; none too few but none too much.

Perry is lesser known than cider, save for that strange old thing in Britain called Babycham, which may sit in the minds of a few older readers. In many ways perry has a clean slate and can build its own identity, unlike cider which has the incumbent mass market of cider defining what it is thought to be. But perry's nature is also more unique, from the vastness and age of its trees, to the extra level of mastery it takes to make well. It is truly not quite like anything else.

↑ A young pear orchard.

# CHAPTER 4

# The Seasons

In many ways you can divide the calendar of cider by the four seasons into which we divide the year. The first three of spring, summer, and fall/autumn each fit fairly comfortably as markers upon which to set out the stages of cider, but in all honesty winter must be coerced if it is actually to fit. This is because the final stage, the actual cider-making itself that happens across the final season, can last many months or even a few years. Sometimes, depending on the apples varieties used and the style of cider made, it can be less than six months, but more often it is a long wait (just as waiting for winter to end can be). It is also in many ways the most dormant stage for the makers themselves. With the heady intensity of pressing apples gone, they hand over to the yeasts, to perform the transformation from juice to cider.

As such, a cider becoming "finished" and ready to drink often overlaps the arrival of the next season. This tail to the cider-makers' calendar, effectively how long they choose to ferment and age a cider, is a thing that often marks out those makers of the finest cider. They give this stage all the time it needs, for the cider to truly become as good as it can be. As the saying goes, good things come to those who wait and cider is yet more evidence of this truth; the maker James Forbes, for example, says that cider made with the Ellis Bitter apple takes a good two years to really "give up the goods" and produce its fullest depth of flavor.

This is particularly true for styles that require aging, for example Traditional Method (also known as the Champagne Method; see page 148) ciders which tend to require at least a year and a half in a bottle before they are ready to be sold. This means a few seasons' vintages can be laid down in wait at the same time, overlapping each other before the first is released. The cost of such time for the maker can be huge—they must wait, having long ago paid for these many bottles. Years can go by before they can sell their cider, and get a return on the money, the time, and the effort they invested in it all those years ago. And only then do they truly know if all the risks they took along the way have paid off. For new makers in particular, each season is a leap of faith—what has been learnt in the years before and from the advice of others will be applied, increasing their trust in themselves, but no two seasons will be the same and so will no two ciders from different seasons. But without this risk you do not get these rewards...

→ Sunrise in the early fall/autumn.

# SPRING

It all begins in spring, as the blossom appears on the trees, folding forth from the buds that appeared on the tail of winter. In Britain apple blossom tends to bloom from April through May. It may be slightly earlier the more southerly you go, or in extreme weather years, and may be slightly later the more northerly you go; this is, of course, set by the rhythms of nature and the warmth of the sun.

This beautiful time of year, with its youthful greens and pure pigmented flowers flexing from winter's brown restraint, is ever more special when you know the spectacle of a cider orchard in full bloom. As a thing to look forward to, it holds a place of paradise in the mind. Imagine being stood amongst two-story-high apple trees that layer into the distance of your view. Bulging branches all adorned with flowers, forming layers of petaled points, which fall and fly about in the wind. I can see why the Japanese have such an appreciation of cherry blossom—it seems baffling that our sensibility to our own orchards is not more finely attuned. Perhaps they once were. I've heard people used to go on blossom tours to the orchards of the West Country in the early 1900s. And in Cornwall, in areas such as the Fowey Valley, the blossom tours would happen by boat, viewing the orchards draped down the hillsides, toward the water's edge. You can imagine the river or estuary holding floating petals as they blow off the trees, eventually drifting out to sea. Even the large, commercially farmed orchards that are so prevalent today are a beautiful sight, trees cascading down the slopes, looking a little like a vineyard but coated in pure pink and white. Dainty, delicate, little flowers, petals in the millions, that can be so bright in the fullness of the sun.

Different varieties blossom at slightly different times, and not all blossom is the same; the exact tones and ratios of each vary, the pink may only be present before the flowers have fully opened or begin so subtley that the blossom appears almost white anyway.

Then you have the nomads, the unbeatable grandeur of the perry pear trees; they blossom in pure white, up to four stories tall, often stood in isolation or well spaced apart. Such a vast tree is hard to miss. Thickly coated, their crisp whiteness would make the people in washing detergent adverts swoon. They tend to blossom before apple trees, and as you drive through Herefordshire at the peak of their bloom, they stand above hedgerows and

↑ Blossom on apple trees.

crest hillsides, in their domes of brilliant white. Cherry blossom is white, but cherry trees rarely grow to this size, so you know that these big trees will be perry pears, perhaps 100 or 200 years old, or even older.

Just like the apple trees, each year they put on this show. But why? To reproduce—the same reason for most excessive displays in nature. All their beauty exists so that their flowers may be pollinated and their fruit may grow, and that the seeds of this fruit may grow into new trees.

Bees are not the only pollinators; other insects are too, but bees are important, not to mention fascinating. Apparently the efforts of bees increase agricultural yields around the world (of all crops, not just apples) by as much as 30 percent. As a result, some cider-makers keep bees in the orchard, to encourage this cycle. Others build "bee hotels," as some of the best bees for a cider-maker to encourage into their orchards are so-called "solitary bees," which live alone. Unlike hive bees, which cover a set territory and return to the hive each night, these solitary bees are prolific pollinators, and they make up around 90 percent of the bee species in Britain.

# SUMMER

Then comes summer, where the pollinated blossom becomes fruit, growing in the richness of the summer sun. Each year the way an apple variety grows, even on the very same tree, varies based on the weather of that season. Affected across the months of their growing, the sun, the rain, and the day- and night-time temperatures all contribute to create slightly different results which will change the cider that is ultimately made.

The ratio of sun to water is a key factor. More sun means higher sugar levels in the fruit (provided the trees also have enough water), which means the apple juice will be able to ferment to a higher level of alcohol, and greater alcohol levels can be a factor in achieving more complex cider. If there has been relatively little rainfall, the percentage of liquid in the fruit will be less and the yield of juice that can be pressed from the apples adversely affected. In wine, slightly stressed vines are often said to produce the best wines, and stressed apple trees are said to make more characterful apples, but only if the trees receive the right amount of water.

The best recipe is said to be rain at night and sun in the day, in order to give the fullest mix of complexity of flavor, sugar levels, and juice yield. The trees, of course, don't go anywhere at night; they sit under the stars and moon, having soaked in the sun the daylight has given them. After the sun goes down, like many of us, they drink, and they do so heavily.

Anecdotally we all know how much any given season can vary from the norm, or compared to past years, but the statistics really underpin just how different the weather can be across the growth period of an apple. For example, in 2018 we had a strange year in England; it was sunny, very sunny in fact. Such that 2018 will sit in the memory as a long summer full of dry grass and high temperatures, to an extent rarely seen in the UK. It will be the benchmark against which coming hot summers are compared, being the joint hottest summer ever in the UK since records began a little over a century ago. Hopefully this is not a record that will keep getting broken year after year in the coming decades. I am writing this just before the new season's cider (from 2018) starts to arrive, but it seems set to be a fascinating season.

The fact that each season will vary, and that different varieties will blossom and ripen at different times in the season depending on weather conditions, means each season's apples are not a carbon copy of the past. Not only will the weather affect how the apples grow as a whole, but variations in timing (blossom, ripening, etc.) of different varieties affect the apple varieties individually, meaning the quantity and quality will also vary. The vagaries of each season change the ratios of what varieties a maker actually ends up having to work with. If frost struck when a certain few varieties were in blossom, killing off their flowers, the maker may have little or none of those varieties to work with, but earlier or later blooming varieties may be plentiful, having missed this cold snap.

Some varieties may have grown particularly well that season, by which I mean the conditions that season may somehow have been conducive to a certain few varieties turning out particularly well. A maker will often say that the juice of one variety is tasting especially good that year, and really look forward to tasting the results in the cider it makes. The specifics of such things however, the details of why a certain variety is tasting particularly good in a given year, is still a thing more known by taste than scientific correlation. Scientific research in the world of wine, and the study of the effect of minor climatic variation on the wine that results, is far ahead of cider; it's often said by some 30 years or more. The science of the mass-market cider-makers is pretty good; it is thorough, but mostly only pertains to certain ends, such as identifying what they consider as faults. I would suggest that the understanding of the effect of many of the factors that play a role in fine cider-making is perhaps even farther behind. Factors like the difference that soil types have on apple-growing and the ciders that result are mostly speculative. There are not enough good makers nor enough collective experience yet to draw any definitive conclusions from the effect of such factors. We know that the differences exist, and how faceted the spectrum is, but not necessarily what correlates a difference in the climate or location, to a flavor in the ciders

→ Apple trees absorb most water through their roots at night.

themselves, beyond basic principles.

In spite of all this variation, what an apple tree can produce in a single summer is rather incredible. In a high-cropping year its branches may hang to the ground, bowing its boughs, and can even be snapped off by the weight of the apples they carry. It is truly amazing just how much fruit a single tree can produce, the ratio of apples to tree seems to defy belief, and all of these apples growing seemingly from nothing, over the space of just a few months.

While all of this happens, animals may be grazed beneath the trees, sheep are most common, but historically cows may be grazed as well. I remember once reading of large apple trees historically having been grafted/budded by someone on horseback, so that the wood attached would be too high for the cattle to eat. Or, crops may have been grown in between the trees, as intensive orcharding of small trees is a somewhat new thing, and trees would have historically been spaced farther apart. And this is a wonderful thing about orchards—they need not be some massive monocultural coercion like so much of agriculture has become today. Farmers back in the 17th century worked in this polycultural manner, and it suited them for another reason: as most cider apples are not harvested until fall/autumn, cider-making was not at odds with their other activities, happening in what were otherwise the slack months of the year. Livestock could graze and find shade under the

apple trees in summer, then be fed in autumn on the pomace left from pressing the apples. This feed, according to John Beale, accounted for the quality of Herefordshire bacon; he claimed it to be the best bacon in the country—perhaps the Iberico pork of England?

← Long summer evenings with cider.

# FALL/AUTUMN

After summer's great efforts, fall/autumn slinks into place. The leaves eventually go orange, turning to amber tones reminiscent of the colors of cider, and then drop to the ground to leave the branches naked, bar any apples still left upon the tree. Fall brings with it picking season, the time to harvest the apples and set them on their way to becoming cider. It is the primary pursuit of this season for any cider-maker and takes substantial and timely effort.

Ripeness is key, and it seems many in the mass market make the mistake of harvesting their fruit too early, favoring ease over allowing the fullest flavor to develop. One of the key factors to ripeness is how much starch in the apple has turned into sugar. You can test for this with iodine, but many of the best makers will simply walk the orchards themselves, to judge from experience when the time is right to pick a specific variety.

Different apple varieties will not become ripe at the same time; indeed, many varieties were selected precisely for cider-making in order to spread out the harvesting time, as more apples can be harvested and more cider made when they don't all become ripe at once. Those that come first are called early picking varieties, those that come late are late picking varieties, and their picking time can vary by as much as four months.

The origin of the term "windfall" refers to when fruit has been blown from a tree by the wind. In particularly dry years apples can fall early, with the stems weak from a lack of moisture in their cells, and a little time on the ground can help the starch in them turn to sugar. And in the 17th century cider-makers would often store the apples once picked or collected for as long as a month or two before pressing.

Which apples you actually use is the next question. Any with rot or that are under-ripe (apples will not all ripen on the same tree all at once) are not what you are looking for. At Little Pomona in Herefordshire for example, they go one step farther, creating four categories for picked apples: grades A, B, C, and D.

When picking apples from the tree itself, tree size makes a difference. There are three key categories of apple tree (as well as others), each a variation in size. First is a full standard tree—the stuff of generations past, these are the giants that can be a few stories high. Then you have half-standards, and finally bush orchards, trees grown on rootstocks that keep the trees small and bush-like in scale. Bush orchards are favored by the growers of apples for the mass market, as they have small flexible trunks which can be shaken by a machine mounted on a tractor, in order to shed the apples from the tree. But for full standard trees, often preferred by the small maker, hand-picking is how things are done, and where necessary a simpler device is used—a long pole with a hook on it called a "panking pole." Apple trees can be large, but when it comes to size perry pears claim the title, as they can be four or more stories tall, with a wide span. The nobility of centuries reaching skyward, they must be some of the largest fruiting trees in the world and they can be tricky to pick, even with a panking pole.

After picking comes pressing. The apples are ground and pressed for their juice, to be entombed in barrels or tanks for metamorphosis into cider. When working with late picking varieties, pressing can run as late as January for some.

→ Pears being harvested at Gregg's Pit using a panking pole.

# WINTER

In winter the cider ferments. Once on its way it is largely a
waiting game, one of giving this fascinating natural process the
time it needs. There are a few exceptions, such as keeving and ice
cider-making, which each have a few extra stages that need to
take place before their fermentations can get under way. But
we will go into these details in the section on Styles (see pages
120–163), as well as the choice of what the cider is fermented in,
and to what end.

Fermentation is affected by the ambient temperature. As a general rule the
yeasts (see page 128) will be more active in warmer temperatures, and will
slow down in colder temperatures. In winter's colder months, a fermentation
can seem to stop almost completely, only to pick up again as the weather
warms. You can see when a fermentation is active by the gases that are
released; to stop too much air getting in and spoiling the cider, air locks are
used on the top of the tanks or barrels, usually using a layer of water that
easily allows gas to escape but no air to get in. The amount of gas released
is substantial, so bubbles can be seen or heard regularly rising up through
these air locks as the pressure is released. It can make a charming noise, these
little burps of bubbles, especially in a room with a good few fermentations,
chattering away.

   There is another choice that the orchardist has at this time of year, one
that will help shape next year's crop: that of pruning. Pruning is often done
in winter, but can also be done at other times in the year. Loosely speaking,
the efforts of the tree can be "directed" either toward growing itself, or
toward growing apples and pruning helps assist this. The old saying was that
you should be able to throw your hat through a well-pruned tree, thanks to
well-spaced branches. Pruning will help keep a tree healthy, removing any
diseased wood, keeping its shape balanced, and keeping it vigorous, with
enough light and air getting to the branches.

   Many varieties can be somewhat biannual, particularly perry pears,
growing lots of fruit one year, then barely any the next. Pruning can also help
with this. At times such biannuality is innate in the variety, but it can be
derived as a pattern from factors such as weather, for example frost at

↑ Walking the orchards of Starvecrow, Sussex, during the winter.

blossom time giving little or no fruit that year.

In winter, bush orchards can look a little like vineyards, gnarled and bare branches writhing in rows. But I often see the odd standard tree dotted about in cider country, with deep red apples hanging on its branches into late December, that one late variety in the orchard that hasn't been picked, or lives as a wildling in a hedgerow. It feels fitting timing in the build-up to Christmas, the leaves having fallen from the tree with only these brightly colored baubles left against the backdrop.

# MULLED CIDER

Winter, of course, has its connotations for the drinker with mulled cider. Way back when, mulling was done in a mix of ways: metal shoes were made, often from copper as it is a great conductor of heat, and the "toes" poked into a fire to heat the liquid they contained. They might resemble a pot or mug with what looks like a duck's beak attached, rather than a shoe, and were used for warming both cider and ales. Hot pokers or swords were also used, with the cider steaming and spitting as the hot poker lost its heat into the liquid.

Mulling for most, of course, suggests adding spices and sweetening the drink, rather than just heating it, and as noted earlier, in the past drinks were often spiced and sweetened to improve them and cover faults. When mulling cider I have found that the best starting point is a dry cider that is then sweetened, giving you the benefits of both dry-complexity and sweetness combined. Toasting the spices will release the oils, giving more vibrancy to your brew. Vanilla adds a nice element to the sweetness, and the final touch, to balance the sweetness, the flavor-enhancing properties of a good pinch of salt, ideally a little smoked salt. A little like adding salt to the rich fruitiness of chocolate—when done in the right moderation it gives yet another thing to play on your taste buds and can really help bring the drink together.

Down in Devon, with Polly and Mat Hilton of Find & Foster (see page 152), we have mulled in a manner more akin to the charms of the past. Taking hot pebbles from the edge of a fire on the beach and spooning them into mugs of cider, it too steams and hisses, and likely adds a little salt, from the spray of the sea cast upon the pebbles. When the hissing has died down and the steaming settled, you know most of the heat has been delivered from the pebble and into the cider, and carefully you drink...

# CIDER SEASON

The "season" of a cider, as listed on the label of the bottle, is the year the fruit was grown. It's used in the same way as the wine term "vintage." As the fruit is the key variation, when it was grown defines "when" the cider dates from. For example, apples grown in 2018 will form the 2018 season cider, and will not be released at the earliest until spring of 2019.

The wait of winter is made all that more tense for the maker in expectation of the first taste of the new season's cider. From this first taste, usually after a few months of fermenting, a maker will know how well that season is shaping up, and if anything individually (such as a single tank or barrel) is tasting particularly good.

For me, it's one of the most exciting and intriguing moments, going to visit a maker and having the first taste of the new season's cider, direct from the tank, with the maker. The cider is still underway, a juvenile thing with a future ahead of it, and by no means finished. But it is incredible to know a cider in this way, from its early signs of potential, through to its final form. And to taste the spectrum of a maker's making, as it stands at that moment in those samples of a season, and to taste just how much different fermentations of exactly the same juice can vary. It truly shows you the complexity and depths that cider-making can hold.

Then the maker begins to consider what they may do with each fermentation, what may become which style, in order to best demonstrate its virtues. This is one of the key rounds of choice, and reflects the most important thing to know about the season: a maker only gets one chance each year to make cider, and so in the life of someone who starts making cider at 20, by the time they are 70 they will have had just 50 seasons, 50 attempts to make cider, to learn from their mistakes of last season, and to get to know the variations they must work with. Of course a maker will produce more than one cider each season, but they will not know how any of these will turn out until the following season, perhaps longer, when the cider is finally ready. And any small variations in their way of making, any tests and experiments will only lead to lessons learnt over a long period of time. So particularly for newer makers, the sharing of knowledge is so very important; the standing on the shoulders of giants that is working together.

And remember that here we are talking about the season of the finest makers of cider; much cider is not made in this way: industrial mass-market cider-makers do not work in this way, and it is of course useful for their ciders to be made quickly. What they produce is intended to be the exact same each year, and can often be made year round, in a near constant flow. So the cider-maker's calendar varies hugely depending on what kind of maker you are.

↓ 2015 season bottles from Oliver's.

# CHAPTER 5

# The Regions

In Herefordshire Cathedral, along with books dating back over 900 years, there is a chained library; many manuscripts held in place by long chains, their metal rings looping down from the shelves give a strange physicality to it all; a limit to how far they can travel and a radius in which their knowledge exists. But perhaps the most amazing thing within the cathedral's walls is the *Mappa Mundi*, a map of the known world at the time of its making in the 1290s. It is the largest medieval map known to still exist.

I first saw the *Mappa Mundi* on a gray and slightly rainy day, wandering inside from a market that was taking place in the churchyard of the cathedral. The map shows the world, but not quite a world we would recognize today, with precision mapping and education having written the shapes of the continents into each of our minds across that well-known, blue-and-green patchwork rectangle. The *Mappa Mundi* shows barely any ocean on its circular world; instead a jumble of continents and rivers extends as far as Gibraltar, in the direction we know today as south. I say known world in the loosest sense: it has paradise to the north, where the north pole would be on a globe, and Noah's Ark just north of the Aegean Sea. Jerusalem sits in the center, the Red Sea and possibly Sri Lanka or Sumatra lie to the northeast. What is now the United Kingdom sits down to the southwest, by the map's edge, the British Isles resembling the form of the fetal position. In total, 420 towns, and 33 animals and plants, are shown, all encased by a thin band of sea at its circled edge.

I find it fascinating that a map includes paradise—the idea that the world extended beyond our understanding, so such possibilities could have existed in an undiscovered corner of the Earth. The idea of paradise in itself is a fascinating thought; author Laurie Lee's thoughts on it were that many of the ideas of paradise, such as those in the Bible, sound like a dull and unentertaining eternity. But in past times the appeal of paradise—as a place where food is naturally abundant, where people are not fighting for survival, and the climate allows ease—is far more understandable. You can see the appeal of such magical longing for our ancestors—long before the easy abundance of industrially produced food we know today, the prospect of never having to worry about your next meal, or the need for shelter, from the hunter-gatherer to the medieval peasant, could indeed have been the stuff of heaven on Earth.

→ The *Mappa Mundi* depicts how the world was believed to look at the end of the 13th century.

# THE IMAGINARY MAP OF CIDER

The *Mappa Mundi* is a window into a different time, and how the world was once seen, and I think of this when I drive down the lanes of Herefordshire, surrounded by the lost world of cider, which has been superseded by the more industrial ways of today. I suppose if I were to draw a map of the known world of cider today, as I imagine it looks through the eyes of the public in Britain, it would look a little like this…

At its heart would be the southwest of England, too often seen as the land of scrumpy. Home to long-bearded men, reminiscent of a pagan past, sat (always sat, or perched at the very least) drinking a vinegary concoction. Then there would be the vast plains of the mass market, such as the territory of Magners to the west, and Bulmers in the center. This land would be a little like the Eurasian steppe, a vast temperate land, a consistent landscape, largely empty but spreading far and wide. At times perhaps turning to desert, like the arid salt flats and sand dunes shown in Strongbow TV adverts. Parents would tell their children tales of a dark corner of the map where they should not explore, the wild lands of white cider. A place roamed by teenagers and tramps, a mix of concrete jungles, the dark recesses of doorways, and forests made up of the lesser used parts of parks.

To the cold north and beyond the shores of Britain would be the sweet fruity concoctions of Sweden! Seeing the midnight sun and covered in winter snows, yet still able to make "cider" with passionfruit in it… Those crazy Vikings, invading from across the North Sea, pillaging supermarkets, pubs, and parks across the land and trading exotic things. Where does this exotic fruit come from? Probably some land far away, at the unknown end of some distant trading route.

For the few lucky enough to have traveled south, there would exist the *cidre* lands of northern France and the *sidra* lands of northern Spain. Fascinating cultures both of them, each with their own ingrained ways of being.

Beyond that, there would be little islands from which boats come, bringing cider to trade. The offerings of South African cider being fairly often seen but little known, traders often bringing only one thing from that dry savannah. The same goes for the islands of New Zealand, from which settlers have seemingly brought a little slice of their culture to the mass market, a moot point for its elders...

There would be some free towns here and there, the realms of new settlements and new ciders. With a good reputation, and signs of hope and progress for a better society, word would be spread of the opportunities that lie in these new towns. Of the promise for a better world they hold. One of greater reward than the existing kingdoms and feudal lords; where the tied contracts of those in power enforce their wills on pubs across the land. Perhaps there would even be some outposts, those one or two who defend their own way and are the stuff of local cider legend, from Celtic tribes to fancy castles and ciders made by the same method as Champagne.

There might be legends and myths, tales told of highly advanced civilizations that crumbled. Perhaps word is spoken of paradise, of the Garden of Eden, a mythical place of exquisite cider. Or of such things as the cider flute of King Arthur, the land of Pomagne, and its since last descendent, Queen Boudica of Babycham. But few know the reality of this past; it has faded into little known legend and each of its tales is a hint of the world that once was, the faintest remnants of great civilizations of cider that have been buried in the passage of time.

← Cider's place in the British countryside is long established.

# REGIONAL DIFFERENCES

To get back to reality, and how the map of cider actually appears today, is to speak of perhaps an equally obscure thing. Just like the voyages across oceans needed to know the surface of the Earth, it can be hard to know the true extent of the world of cider if you do not delve into its depths. To know it you must explore. But when your radar extends far enough, and you have explored vast oceans, you start to see how the map might look, and it is a fascinating thing. As not only is the history of cider, but also its present state, being rediscovered and redefined, as are many other things in the galaxy of alcohol.

There are two key differences that shape the regions we will look at—environmental differences and cultural differences (and I am including both geographical and climatological differences within environmental).

The first thing to know about environmental differences is that apples or pears of a variety do not all grow the same in different places, and the cider they make therefore varies. The climate of a specific region, as well as the soils and altitude, creates variations in the fruit as it grows in that specific region. This might sound subtle, but the differences in the wider scheme of things are pronounced and give different regions very different ciders. This will often define what varieties grow best and so become the focus of cider-making in a given region.

Differences formed by the specifics of a region's own locale (the environmental factors for that specific region, often called terroir in wine) set the boundaries of what varieties can be grown well, or grown at all, in that region. But as with the vagaries of the season, regional differences are pronounced and exist across a vast array of possibilities. I can tell you the objective elements that we do know, but the key things I cannot tell you are why many of these are as they are. Knowledge of the causation of such differences are a thing the future hopefully holds. But the key thing I want to impart from my experience of different regions is just how much things can vary, from the apples grown within a single orchard, to the ciders made across the entire globe.

The most fascinating question then comes: if such factors become better known in cider and enough makers start making to a caliber that makes the locale from which the cider came evident, how broad—as well as nuanced—might the spectrum then be?

For now, it is hard to truly convey in words just how much regions vary based on their different environments. This is largely as cider-making on the whole is still such a homogenized thing, that any reflections of location are often lost to more universal intentions (such as heavy industrial intervention). Quite simply, the playing field is far from flat. In fact it is a vast minefield, running from minimal intervention at one end, to the industrial in aspiration at the other, even within the small-batch side of making. But some things are incredibly clear: how incredibly different the ciders made on either side of this little country I call home archetypally are, for example. Also how incredibly different the varieties that are historically grown in different regions can be, too.

One of the greatest examples of just how much different locales can vary seems to be made evident by how differently the very same varieties grow in different regions. For me, one of the clearest ways to experience such variation has been by tasting how incredibly different ciders can be, despite having been made in similar ways, with the same single or dominant variety, simply in different regions. But this does make sense when you think of the differences of environment affecting the fruit: the effect of micro-climates and localized variations such as rain shadows, specific altitude, proximity to the coast, pitch of the land, soil variation, wind patterns, orientation, and sunlight hours. For example, Little Pomona in Herefordshire (see page 143) has an orchard sat predominantly on red clay (as many of the orchards in Herefordshire are), but a rockier shelf runs through part of the orchard, underneath many of their Dabinett trees. The orchard is south-south-west facing, sat on a fairly gentle slope, with a good steady breeze running through it (which helps prevent fungal diseases), and with a lot of exposure to the sun. All can play their part in affecting the outcome of the apples they grow and the cider they make. Such is how specifically the environment can vary within even a single orchard.

Such nuances of locale were known in past eras; for example John Beale (1608–1683) wrote: "He that would treat exactly of *cider* and *perry*, must lay his foundations so deep as to begin with the soil." Much of Herefordshire holds the deep red of the old sandstone that underlies it, often forming a clay soil on the surface. There are exceptions, such as the silurian shale of the Woolhope Dome, around the village of Woolhope, and certain soils were historically favored for the varieties they grew and the ciders these made, at times to a very specific degree; the locale of an individual village could be prized, and certain soil types were warned against.

But of course regardless of how exceptionally varied, locale-specific, and seasonally variable the fruit of an apple tree is, it is only as good as what you do with it. Chucking it in with thousands of others from orchards spread far and wide and then turning this into concentrate will negate almost all of any difference that did exist (which of course is the point of such methods, consistency). But variety can be consistent: it can be of a consistently high quality, and it can be consistently exciting by virtue of its variation, let alone the consistent refinement of the skill of the maker, season after season, by evidence of the ciders they make. Knowing a consistency of quality that is reached regardless of all of these variations and is expressive of the locale from which it came, now that is a special thing.

But environmental elements are not the only factor affecting how varieties are grown and cider made; culture destines it to not be. And as a result many historic cider-making regions have distinctive aspirations and properties to the ciders they make. Built up over time, and taking the result of their locales' prevailing environmental factors as the starting point, certain characteristics have been prized. And where culture is concerned we will speak of specific countries.

↘ Apple trees growing in Devon,
discovered by Find & Foster.

# SPAIN

The Spanish culture of *sidra* centers on Asturias and the Basque Country. Sat close to the northern Atlantic coast of that grand peninsular, bordering the Bay of Biscay and surrounded to the south by a barrier of mountains, this enclave appears a green and luscious land from the air, unlike so much of Spain. The culture of *sidra* is fascinating, as is so much of the culture of Spain; it has a depth unto its own, a prizing of theater over mere function.

The cider itself is usually high in a certain form of acidity—volatile acidity—with *Sidra Natural* its traditional form. In more recent times, other methods and styles have been increasingly exercised, but this natural form holds many delights; it is fermented with wild yeasts (see page 128), from nothing but the juice of the apples pressed, it is still and dry; this ethos has minimal intervention written into its nature. It is served in small measures by being

poured from as great a height as possible, to invigorate the carbon dioxide naturally dissolved in the cider and give it a creamy texture, softening its acidity. The acidity, of course, comes from the predominant varieties in the region, and the practice of this making goes back many generations, such that *sidrerias* are wonderfully ingrained in and around places like the coastal city of Gijón. Huge chestnut barrels were historically used for the fermentations, and even today, though steel tanks might often have replaced them, you might find yourself upon a visit drinking this most noble form of cider straight from the tank, a small tap on its vast belly jetting it creamily into your glass.

But when you are not at the place of its making, the *sidra* comes by the bottle, poured by the skill of the *escanciador*, the server of cider. They reach their arms as wide as their bones allow, one down low with the glass, the other up high with the bottle, to pour with great skill a steady trickle of the liquid. Once it is poured, you the drinker cannot wait around—you must drink it before its creamy texture settles back to its acidic calmer self.

It's a glorious thing, and such a uniquely characterful way of drinking, so much so that around 95 percent of the *sidra* made in Asturias is also drunk there; I don't know that you can replicate such thorough culture, and the skill of the server it requires, with ease. In Spain, with their knowledge of how to live well and not rush things, it works. But anyone who has queued to be served at a bar in Britain or America can guess why it does not travel more. It also does not fit with the easy and sweet cider that has come to dominate much of the mass market in other regions. You have to go to Spain to truly taste this cider. And if you do, taste it with the wonderful local food.

← Spanish cider is usually poured from a distance in order to encourage the release of carbon dioxide.

# FRANCE

Where in Spain an ethos reigns supreme, in Normandy in France it is a style that has become king. Known as *keeving* to the English tongue, but also as the *Normandy Method*, the technique itself is something we will go into in more detail in the chapter on Styles (see page 121). In essence, this is an old method, dating back to the 1600s or even earlier. It is a technical method and takes great skill and understanding from the maker to do well, and by its nature some of the sugars naturally in the juice are retained without the cider fermenting fully to dry. This means the ciders of this region are often low in alcohol, at times as little as 2 percent.

Normandy and Brittany are the two regions on the north coast of France that claim French cider-making for their own. The ciders of Brittany tend to be drier and higher in alcohol than those of Normandy, and its soils are said to contain granite, giving more minerality to the region's ciders. After a fall from grace of fine cider-making in Britain during the 18th century, it was France which became the bastion of good cider, and as such the culture of cider-making here can border on the château culture of wine. To give those who know little of cider in France, or of these regions in particular, an idea of the extent of the history of cider-making that once existed here, until the end of the 19th century France is said to have had the largest acreage of apple trees of any nation on Earth, and some one million people were estimated to have been employed in cider-making. Supposedly in this era, France drank more cider than wine.

But in spite of this past, today cider plays second fiddle to wine in France, and it is often Calvados that is prized far beyond cider itself. Calvados is cider brandy, hailing from the Calvados region in Normandy. It's not something we've yet touched on, but of course cider can be distilled. It can be a fascinating spirit, full of the flavor of its fruit in spite of an alcohol level of 40 percent or more. In Calvados it's often drunk during a large meal, to dampen the sense of a full belly and make room for more food. There is no other region in the world that holds anywhere near the note for cider brandy that Calvados does; in Britain in the 17th century distilling cider gained some—but not especially substantial—traction, at times being blended with cider to create a drink titled "Royal Cider." *Pommeau* is a similar thing, but one that is still very much alive in France; it is a blend of cider brandy with apple juice, resulting in a drink a little under 20 percent alcohol.

With the above being said, and the New Wave rising in cider, there are a few fascinating examples of French cider-makers that are forging a new path, reflecting bygone glories, and exemplifying a new respect for cider in its own right.

It's no surprise that cider-making in both France and Spain is centered nearly exclusively on their temperate northern coasts. The heavy sun and harshness of more southerly climes may suit vines, but not so much apples. Thanks to these regions, each of these countries has a distinctive archetypal style of cider—in fruit, ethos, and aspiration. The United Kingdom, however, is a bit more of a mixed bag.

→ Cider pairs well with traditional French food, such as cheese and charcuterie.

# UK

Cider is made almost all over the UK, even in Scotland and the northern counties of England. And while the southwest may be known as cider's spiritual home, and there are certain archetypes to the cider made there, no single style or ethos has come to dominate good-quality cider-making in the manner it has in France or Spain. As already noted, here in Britain a certain divide can be made, drawn roughly down the middle of the country, based on the apples of the east coast and the west coast (see page 70). In more detail, you might describe the two regions of this divide as the West Country and the South East Coast, as such is where they are really centered. On the South East Coast we predominantly have acid-focused ciders, and in the West Country we often have higher tannin ciders. But looking at ciders based on these two properties is something we'll come back to in the section on Drinking and Dining (see pages 164–179), as these two properties, their presence or absence, roughly apply across all ciders, and help describe what a cider is like.

In spite of this divide, each of the many cider-making areas in Britain will have its own locale, and often be rich in a history that informs its present-day cider-making. As John Beale wrote in the 17th century in his *Aphorisms Concerning Cider*:

"*I cannot undertake to particularize all kind of Soil, no more than to compute how many syllables may be drawn from the Alphabet; the number of Alphabetical Elements being better known than the Ingredients and Particles of Soil, as Chalk, Clay, Gravel, Sand, Marle, (the tenaciousness, colour, and innumerable other qualities, showing endless diversties).*"

And as such it should be remembered just how much variation there can be within locales in each of these regions. But where the finest cider was concerned, Beale said that:

"*I cannot divine what Soil or what Fruit would yield the best Cider; or, how excellent Cider or Perry might be if all Soils in common and all Fruit were tried;*

*but for thirty years I have tried all sorts of Cider in Herefordshire, and for three years I have tried the best Cider in Somersetshire; and for some years I have had the best Cider of Kent and Essex at my call; yet hitherto I have always found the Cider of Herefordshire the best, and so adjudged by all good Palates."*

## HEREFORDSHIRE

We've touched upon Herefordshire quite a lot already, and with good reason—it has an incredible history and many wonderful things are currently happening there. But it is also the largest cider-making county in the largest cider-producing country in the world (although most of this is, of course, rather lifeless industrial cider).

The name Hereford—the capital city of the county—in old English means "Army Crossing," as it was a place to ford the River Wye, but the rest of the county beyond its ancient city walls is a quieter place, sat in western England, and bordering Wales, supposedly way back when the battling of tribes for this border region cast the die for the few large settlements that exist there today, meaning it is a spacious place, rife with some of the best agricultural land in the country and scattered with market towns. It is a land of grand valleys, and distant views across to the smooth tops of the Welsh mountains. It is a little like what the Americans call "fly-over country," but in an unaware sense, more simply passed by in ignorance, with the M5 motorway sliding past and the often favored destinations of the Cotswold hills to the east and Wales off to the west.

→ Herefordshire makes more cider than anywhere else in the UK.

Much of the county has rich red clay soils; when the fields have been plowed they can look like maroon crevasses, with cracked ridges of waxy clay rising like jagged ice. But the main thing you come to know of Herefordshire cider is its apples; it is a heartland of many of the finest traditional cider apples, rife with tannic complexity and localized nuance. At their best, these are rich, complex, multi-layered ciders. Historically, Herefordshire has long been known for the complexity of its cider, as well as their aging potential, and where its finest creations today are concerned the same holds true; they can be some of the richest and most complex ciders made anywhere. It can be thought of as a little like the Bordeaux of the cider world. If anywhere on Earth holds great potential to be the leading light in the world of fine cider, given its history and the sheer number and quality of orchards it holds, it is Herefordshire; but the region has its industrialized makers (and on the other end of the spectrum, at times a farm-gate simplicity) to win over or supercede first, which is no small challenge.

## DEVON

In the recorded words of the past heyday of cider, alongside Herefordshire, Devon is the other most famous region for fine cider-making in Britain. These are the places reputed to have made the most refined and most prized ciders. Devon today does not have the scale of cider-making of Herefordshire, especially not in industrial makers, but this slightly cleaner slate has given its New Wave makers a chance to set the reputation of Devon cider as a superior thing.

While there are fewer fine makers than in the likes of Herefordshire, the history is there and so are the environmental factors. Like much of Herefordshire, the Devon Redlands region holds a base of red sandstone, meaning makers such as Find & Foster (see page 152), just outside Exeter, exist in a pocket of red soils. I note this more for the sake of similarity than to claim it is a superior soil, as coincidence is rarely a cautious thing. But while this element may be similar, Devon's south coast gets notably more

↑ Dusk in Devon.

sunlight hours on average than the more northerly Herefordshire, but its proximity to the sea helps moderate the temperature, so the average temperature of Herefordshire in summer is actually higher than more southerly Devon.

Historically, the method of *Keeving* (see page 154) is said to have had some prominence in Devon; also being known as the Normandy Method, the proximity of these two places across the English channel giving rise to a use of a similar style of cider-making makes a lot of sense.

Sinking to the sea on its south coast, the short, sharp valleys of this part of Devon hold a unique character as they drop down to flat valley bases and out into the estuaries and sea. And when the summer comes, or even when it doesn't, it is certainly a most beautiful and fitting place to drink cider; in the warmth of the south coast, with seafood as your cider pairing.

## SOMERSET

Somerset is seen by many, in Britain especially, as the heartland of cider. It is the custodian of a certain form of making, often one reminiscent of a somewhat bucolic past, that of farmhouse cider and a way of the countryside and of farming now long gone. But it is the home of many of the best traditional cider apples— some of my favorites, such as the Yarlington Mill (see page 75), stem from its grand history of cider-making—as well as some amazing voices in New Wave cider.

In my experience, tannic though its fruit can be, the majority of its ciders are at their best a softer, mellower thing than those of Herefordshire. More the Burgundy to Herefordshire's Bordeaux perhaps, they have a sumptuous ease, perfectly at home with its soft rolling hills and pastoral summer bliss.

Much of its orcharding happens on the slopes in the Somerset Levels, between its various hills, such as the Mendip, Blackdown, and Quantock Hills. Its bedrock is mainly sandstone, with limestone forming some of these hills.

## THE SOUTH EAST COAST

Comprising Sussex, Hampshire, Kent, and farther north up the east coast, Suffolk and Norfolk, this part of the country gets more sunlight hours than any other region in the UK. However, the varieties grown there do not tend to reach the sugar levels of the traditional cider apples of the West Country, and so do not create such high levels of alcohol. Higher levels can be reached if more sugar is added to fuel the fermentation, such as in a secondary fermentation as is used for Traditional Method sparkling ciders (see page 148), which the apples of this region lend themselves to very well. In fact, the regions along the south coast could be the Champagne region of cider, much of it even containing the same free-draining chalk substrate and soils as the Champagne region in France. And as I've already noted, I think of apples such as those that dominate in this part of the country (non-traditional cider apples, low in tannin, high in acid) as making the white wines of the cider world.

## OTHER REGIONS TO NOTE

I would be doing them a disservice if I did not mention that some wonderful enclaves of cider- and perry-making are happening in many other parts of the country, such as Wales, Cornwall, Gloucestershire, Worcestershire, and Dorset. These regions may not have the historical clout of those we have spoken of in more depth, and may be yet to establish their fullest identity, or even know the finest form the apples of their region can make, but each shows signs of wonderful possibilities.

And also to note: some would say the West Country of England does have an overarching archetypal style, perhaps one defined mostly by its scrumpies, but to apply this so broadly to all of the West Country I find unfitting; far more happens here than simply the making of this rougher concoction. It may have a certain reputation when coming from these parts, but scrumpy can be made in many places, and is often defined by its lack of finesse over its reflection of a locale.

I've mentioned how Scotland is emerging as another fascinating region, but must stress just how recent and exciting this is. Scotland is a unique landscape, often one of estates, conjuring up the echoes of the wine estates of France… But it's also a big and varied landscape, with possibilities that these pioneering Scottish cider makers are truly making the most of. It will be intriguing to see what Scottish cider becomes in the next 10 years; its challenges may differ in some ways from many English makers to the south—often making their cider far from the benefits of big cities—but with other opportunities at their fingertips.

Also in Wales, where I've mentioned the cataloging and discovery of specifically Welsh cider apple varieties, many of them new discoveries. It's easy to imagine (if you have ever visited the Welsh valleys and beautiful hills that create them) the unique growing conditions that can exist in orchards in Wales—and hence the incredible array of varieties available to the cider makers at Welsh Mountain Cider!

→ The United Kingdom is small compared to many nations, but its landscapes are still so varied.

# USA

Fascinating things are happening in cider in the USA. The market is very small compared to such things as beer, but it is growing fast, having increased in size by around 500 percent since 2011. And things are really only just getting going; without such a continuous history of widespread making as the old European cider nations, it is unburdened by its own past. It is the place of the greatest growth and most intriguing freedom in cider-making. While this brings a mixed bag, it holds many things to be envied. Like the renaissance in American wine-making, it's fascinating to see what such freedoms allow and it should not be underestimated.

The first thing to remember is that the USA is a vast place; its regions are much farther apart than those in the likes of the UK, and the variation of environments it has vary hugely with this. The winters in its northern states can be more akin to the Scandinavian countries in Europe, and summer down south can be akin to the climate of the Mediterranean, or even the North African nations.

This vast nation of pioneering spirit forms the setting for many wonderful things in cider, and they are happening fast. Making is happening all over, but three regions have made themselves especially prominent: New York State, the Finger Lakes, and Vermont in the North East; Washington and Oregon in the North West; and Michigan and the Great Lakes more centrally. There are many other pockets of cider-making, across the country, but these three regions have become the most prominent.

To learn a little more about how cider is shaped in the United States, we turn to a few native voices, each fine cider-makers of note in their own right:

## • MAKER: **ELEANOR LÉGER, EDEN SPECIALTY CIDERS, VERMONT, NEW ENGLAND**

"I think what's very distinctive about American cider, and the American cider market as a whole, is that it didn't exist in any significant way until 2011. Now, all of sudden, we have everything at once; you have a ton of different things happening, flavored ciders, people making cider that fits into the craft beer market, as well as wine-like ciders; it's all over the place. There are about 900 cideries in the USA now, and there are probably around 50 that look to make cider in the kind of manner that we do. If you look at it by volume, cider is teeny, its 0.46 percent of the total alcoholic drinks market in the US, and likely less than 10 percent of this is the kind of heritage cider-making that we do—but we don't really know because it's really hard to measure.

"What motivates me is the apples, the amazing heritage apples as we have very few. In the US we produce 250 million bushels [a bushel is a measure equal to 8 gallons in capacity] a year of grocery-store apple varieties, there might be 500,000 bushels of various heirlooms and old-style culinary fruit that are grown by people that just love them. Then there might be less than 100,000 bushels of tannic cider fruit. So whereas in Britain you have a surplus of tannic cider fruit, in the US we have barely any. The vast majority of the ciders being made in the US use leftover grocery-store apples and add all kinds of flavors; peach and ginger and all sorts. These are playing to a young market that grew up on sodas and flavored drinks, it's totally normal to them.

↓ Fall/autumn in upstate New York can be an amazingly colorful thing.

"I think when we started, we had CiderCon eight years ago [CiderCon is an annual conference of talks, tastings, and events, that bring makers from all over the world together in the US] and we didn't really feel there were regional styles, but now there absolutely are; in the Pacific North West you are talking ciders with all kinds of crazy things in them, and while there are some great heritage cider-makers in the North West, they are drowned out by the volume of these flavored ciders.

"The fruit growing in Washington state is four times the scale of New York state, which is the second largest region. Then in New England, where we're based, there has been a much longer tradition of cider-making, and it's persisted throughout the years. You have certain key individuals who have made a huge difference, and there are many more small cider-makers who are making heritage wine-style ciders. So there's definitely now a distinction between North East and North West, and Michigan is probably more like the North West, Virginia probably more like the North East, but that's a gross generalization, everything can be found in each region. But there are more of what we call heritage cider-makers in the North East than any other regions; it's down to the history and localities of the place.

"Even when you're making cider like wine there's such a broad spectrum, and the natural wine movement is also broadening that spectrum. What I'm excited about, coming from a wine point of view, is thinking about the fruit. The different heirloom culinary varieties, both North American and European tannic apple varieties, and using cider-making to express the qualities of these varieties; the flavors, the aromatics, the phenolics, in ways that go really well with food. And that's still a really broad range of things; it can be dry, still, and tannic, and high acid, or it can be light and very bubbly, like rose water with lemon. You can have a whole lot of variation, and this is where I have fun as a cider-maker, saying let's do something Riesling-like in style today, and then let's go after Provence rosé tomorrow.

"In New England, we have very lumpy topography, so big-scale orchards are not possible, unlike for example in New York State where you can have large orchards. It limits what we can grow, the quantities we can grow, and the kinds of apples we can grow. In New England, the history of colonization is the oldest; for example the Roxbury Russet apple has been around since 1640. There are probably only 60 acres of it in existence, and if that disappears, that's the end of it. I really want to showcase those apples, so for me cider-making is about how do I bring those flavors out, and a lot of it is through blending.

"When you're thinking about cider like wine, you're thinking about food pairing. I would say that most of us in the US appreciate tannin for structure but not tannin to the degree that you have in the UK where sometimes it can be overpowering to food. We have limited access to tannic apples, and as a result I think we don't yet have the appetite for highly tannic ciders, except on a very limited basis for geeks. So tannin as a component for structure and body, and bringing the fruit forward, is the way I would say those of us who are making cider like wine think about it.

"I'm all about natural wine-making and natural cider-making, but with an understanding of what it takes to make something that is really expressive of the fruit. I'm not doctoring it so I can get it out to market in six months. I might use commercial yeast and sulfur most of the time, it's all of the other stuff in the laboratory handbook that I want to avoid, like enzymes, fining agents, tannin from a bag, etc.

"As an example, we make a still cider from apples grown just in our biodynamic orchard, high acid, high tannin, and we're also in a very cold climate, so by the time we're pressing the apples and putting the juice into the tank it's October and we're already seeing snow. We had an October 19th a few years ago that was 17°F (-8°C), so I'm not dealing with warm temperatures. We just put the juice in tank and let it go on a spontaneous fermentation, we lower the lid and let it sit on its lees and then rack it into a bottle, no sulfur, no filtration, nothing. It takes 2–3 years until it's really ready to drink. In Burgundy, for example, the rule of thumb used to be 2–3 years for white wine, 3–5 for red wine, if you're not manipulating, not fining, not enzyming, etc., if you have real fruit and you're going to wait until it expresses itself. I feel that this cider is an example of a similar kind of craft, and I get really excited about that! This is the ambition, to create ciders that are reflective of where they are from and the quality of the fruit."

• MAKER: **RYAN BURK, ANGRY ORCHARD HARD CIDER, WALDEN, NEW YORK**

Here is Ryan's story, in his own words:

"We definitely have an acid element, especially on the East Coast of the US, that the UK does not use. I think in the long term it probably is a part of what makes us special; that acidity and those chosen apples. There's not a continuity in taste profile of the finer makers across the States, but there is a continuity in intention. We're really just starting to get into this as an industry, to connect makers of certain intentions all across the country in meaningful ways.

"There are more cider-makers in New York than in any other state in the

← One of the cider houses at Angry Orchard.

Union, and we have this really nice mineral-driven acidity, especially in upstate New York. As a general rule, we're going to be making medium to dry ciders, and most people in the area are making drier cider than across the rest of the country. I think it is part of our story, and it's what New York makers are trying to drive forward.

"I am an East Coast cider-maker in this regard, as across the North East, from Vermont all the way down to New York, we share a lot of the same varieties, have the same climates, and share a lot of the same history. We're all very tied to bittersweet apple varieties, and in New York because of the Finger Lakes we've got a nice wine community established that we get to learn from and be a part of, as well as be judged against.

"There are other places across the region that can do a similar thing to us, some of it's happening in Washington, Oregon, Canada, for example. In these places there are makers with the same heritage intentions, that want to define a sense of place, and to look at the history and use it to define their own future.

"For me, a perfect cider is balanced with tannins, and I think on a perfect vintage most New York ciders are going to be somewhere between 7 and 8% alcohol; that's going to be reflective of a really nice year. In a perfect world everyone would be making still cider, but it's not a perfect world. But you'll find that any heritage producer in the area, probably in all of the northeast, is making both still and sparkling ciders."

# REST OF THE WORLD

The extent to which cider is now being made around the world is truly global, sitting mostly in the northern and southern temperate bands, often overlapping the wine-making regions of the world and pushing where they cannot into colder climes. In Canada, for example, Ice Cider (see page 158) has a perfect place to call home, and the Québécois standard holds the quality of its making at a very high level. It sets a charter of how ice cider should be made, and includes a substantive list of all the things that cannot be done, added, or bastardized. But there are also many, many other wonderful styles of ciders being made in Canada, especially on the southeast and southwest coasts, and often in close conversation with their neighbors to the south, the United States.

There is absolutely no chance I can do justice to all of the fascinating and incredible cider making going on across the world here, so my apologies to the makers and regions missed. But as the briefest of examples, to give you a taste, beyond the UK, France, Spain, Canada, and the USA, some other regions from which I have tasted or come across some fascinating ciders these past few years include: Japan, Latvia and a number of other Baltic states, South Africa, Australia, New Zealand, Sweden, Norway, Finland, a couple of corners of South America, Ukraine, Germany, Belgium, Luxembourg, Poland, Ireland, Italy, and various corners of the Mediterranean! Each alone could likely warrant an entire book; if not today then definitely in 10 years time…

→ The best ice ciders are often made in the cold parts of the world.

# CHAPTER 6

# Styles

Before we delve into the different styles
of cider, we must first look at a few
overarching choices the maker has to
make. They are the precursors to style,
if you will, and what follows are some
of the most important questions facing
the cider-maker.

# JUICE CONTENT

We are, of course, still talking about small-batch cider-making, in a manner akin to wine-making, rather than mass-market cider which as we know can be made from as little as 35 percent apple juice concentrate. As such, our focus is entirely on the juice of the apples used, in all its natural complexity. Therefore the aspiration we are holding in highest regard is 100 percent fresh juice. No concentrate, no water, no backsweetening (adding in sugar or unfermented juice to sweeten the cider, or keeved cider, after the fermentation has finished).

Commercial pressures might not always currently allow even some of the best cider-makers to always stick entirely to this aspiration, but it is the goal, the most highly regarded hope.

← The palate of the maker is one of his or her most powerful assets.

# SINGLE VARIETY OR A BLEND?

When the cider-maker is using the juice of just a single variety of apple, the cider is called a single-variety cider. The opposite of, or alternative to, a single-variety cider is of course a blend—a mix of different apples, blended together.

There are virtues to both approaches. The idea of the blend is complexity; you can add layers and tune and tweak the taste of a cider by virtue of what you put in it and at what ratio. Single-variety ciders do not allow this, they are what they are—according to the variety the maker uses and how it grew that year—but what they are can be uniquely characterful. In the heyday of cider in Britain, back in the 17th and 18th centuries, it seems likely from records that the preference where fine cider was concerned was for single-variety ciders. Such was the fame of cider made with the Redstreak apple, for example, and little mention is recorded of blending.

While such single-variety ciders may not have the layered complexity that can be achieved in a blend, the variety that they can have compared to each other can be wonderful and fascinating. The individual character of that variety can be tasted in all its glory, and you the drinker can choose from the broad spectrum of characters this creates; you can tailor what single-variety you drink to the weather, the food you are eating, simply what properties you fancy. A smooth and rounded single-variety cider can sometimes be the most glorious thing, so complex blending is not always the answer. And as the spectrum would suggest, not all single-variety ciders will be smooth and rounded; they can also be incredibly pronounced. Not all varieties lend themselves to a single-variety approach: a variety such as the Foxwhelp (see page 75) has incredibly high levels of acid, so to drink it alone as a single-variety can be near unpalatable, yet it makes for a most wonderful blending tool, bringing a fascinating hit of rhubarb-like tartness to a cider.

The spectrum of single-variety ciders exists either side of blending, extending to the fullest extremes of the apples themselves, and how much they vary, from the fullest acidity apples or the most tannic, not softened by blending, to the very mellowest.

I recently helped (barely) with the season's creation of the Oliver's Vintage Blend, a fascinating cider made from a blend of fermentations coming from up to 16 separate barrels, each having had a minimum of 18 months in oak. It's a surreal task to undertake—you have to taste the cider from each barrel and gain a picture of its properties and hold them in your head (or on paper), and then consider which of those tasted may go together well when combined, before testing combinations; one may be very fruity on the start of the palate but then fade off and have a fairly quiet tail, while another may be quite quiet on the start of the palate, but have a fascinating tail and aftertaste, and so they may combine well, to give greater complexity across the whole palate than either has alone. This description simplifies things a fair bit, but does give you the picture; when you consider that you have 16 barrels to choose from, and can use or not use any ratio of each of the ciders they contain, the number of possibilities is endless. It makes me think of the often touted statistics of the number of moves in chess. You are setting out on a journey on which you cannot try all options, not by a long shot.

One way to go about blending, and one that is practiced by many wonderful makers and is often done in the world of wine, is to blend a small number of varieties, such as three or four, to gain more complexity in the cider but let the characters of each still be prominent. They may also use fermentations that have come from different containers for this, to add extra layers. The key for such simple blending lies in a clever choice of the varieties and fermentations used, and their ratios. As a result, the maker can get a bit of the best of both: the complexity of blending, as well as a cider that still holds a truly unique character. As the saying goes, less is more, but it can be hard to do a simpler blend such as this well. Again, it all comes back to the skill of the maker and their decision-making.

The ciders of James and Susanna Forbes, of Little Pomona in Herefordshire (see page 143) are a great example of this: their 2016 season blend charmingly named "Old Man & the Bee," after the farmer who planted the orchard and the bees that pollinate the fruit (the two key characters in the apples being grown) contained: Harry Masters Jersey (75%), Dabinett (11%), Foxwhelp (9%), and Ellis Bitter (5%). Or their 2015 season blend titled "The Art of Darkness," which saw a long time in the dark before it saw the light of day (one year in tank, one year in barrel, and then six months in bottle), contained: Ellis Bitter (85%), Harry Masters Jersey (9%), and Foxwhelp (6%).

And here we've hit upon an important point: blending does not just involve the blending of several varieties; other points of difference can constitute a blend. Such as blending two different barrels, even if they contain the same variety (as they will almost inevitably taste slightly different). Or blending ciders from varying containers, such as some from stainless-steel tank and some from barrel. They can blend fermentations whose fruit came from more than one orchard, and thus different locales, or simply different batches that may have been pressed at a slightly earlier or later time or have simply turned out differently.

But inevitably, where blended ciders are concerned, there are two sides to the coin. Certain elements of similarity can arise from blending, as a blend will be an aggregate in taste of all of the varieties, containers, etc. that went into it. So while for the small maker blending can yield complexity, in the mass market it can often result in something bland and homogenized. If a maker uses too many varieties in a blend, they can end up with a cider that can be similar to any other such blend; like mixing too many colors in a paint set, the brightness of each color added will be lost and the result will tend toward the same outcome: gray.

It's also likely that mass-market makers working in such a way, with such massive blends, will only use one type of container, such as stainless-steel tanks, or only one strain of inoculated yeast (see page 128), for all of their fermentations. So again, variety is limited and the cider will all trend to a middle ground, an average.

The art of blending is not to over-do it, and instead use the specific character of different varieties and fermentations, to make something that is more complex and greater than the sum of its parts. Not just a job lot of varieties that have been blindly thrown together, and will trend to the same result: one that lacks distinctive character.

→ Tasting different batches before blending is a fascinating process.

# HOW TO BLEND CIDER

There are two main ways a cider-maker can actually go about blending: before or after the cider has been fermented. It's widely known that it is best to blend once the cider has been fermented, if you are to blend with the greatest nuance as it gives the maker more control over the final outcome. If a maker ferments each variety that might go into a blend separately, they are then able to taste all of these finished ciders and combine small samples of each cider to test different blends and perfect the ratios they will use. This allows an incredible degree of finetuning to be done: you can tweak the ratios of each cider being put in the blend to a degree as precise as 1 percent or so. You then take the blend you have chosen from these small-scale tests, and apply the same ratios of each cider to a full batch for bottling.

The other way a maker can go about it is blending before the juice has been fermented into cider. A good maker will do this by the taste of the fresh pressed juice and knowledge of previous similar blends done in previous years. The maker can choose ratios of how much of each variety to use, or even do variables thereof, but once they have combined these juices what they cannot do is undo the blend. All they can do is blend it further, by blending it with more juice or cider. They do not have the freedom allowed to a maker who fermented each variety separately and then works out their blend with small-scale tests.

Often blending at the stage of pressing like this will be done for convenience. Unless a maker has variable capacity tanks, they cannot underfill a tank or barrel, as doing so would allow too much oxygen to interact with the fermentation. So if you only have a small amount of a certain single variety—less than a full tank for example—the maker may have to blend it. Or equally, if a small amount of juice from a certain variety is left after a few tanks have been filled, the options are either to throw it away or to blend it.

But blending for convenience like this can also exist on a whole other scale and can be a driving force for larger cider-makers. A medium- or large-sized maker will use far greater volumes of fruit than a small one, and so may have to take a greater range of varieties, from a greater number of orchards. Getting large amounts of just a few varieties may not always be possible, nor practical. But I tend to get suspicious of blends containing huge numbers of varieties, for example 40 or 50 different varieties, as it suggests the maker is simply favoring convenience over nuance of taste. Often such makers may proclaim on the label that the cider is "made of

XX number of apple varieties," as though more is inherently better—such is the world of marketing... While there are some makers who might work with such nuance, or simply create some exquisite ciders with a blind blend of many varieties, I have found that such complex blends are the end result of convenience.

Such methods are understandable, as availability thanks to that season's harvest, from multiple suppliers, can become a complex thing for a bigger maker. But a little like the hegemonic results of concentrate use, this "throwing everything in together" creates a more monotone result. The

↑ Blending is an intuitive skill.

variation that a single apple variety brings to the blend, even if 100 percent juice is used, is to a degree negated by the volume of others in the blend; add or subtract a variety or two from a blend of 50, and unless they were one of the predominant varieties present, the overall taste of the blend will only change in a minor way. This manner of making is good for consistency, but not for character.

Some in the world of cider hold the view that a blended cider is the ideal, that blending can create a perfectly balanced cider, or that certain apple varieties, such as the Kingston Black, hold such a balance as a single variety. But I've always found this quite a narrow view; it holds a single vision of what quality is in cider, and in my view is a kind of thinking that is unwittingly taking a similar line to the mass market and negating the virtues of variety.

# WILD YEASTS OR AN INOCULATED YEAST?

A thing I find most intriguing, and it's not only the humility of a wonderful man, is the simplicity with which Tom Oliver always describes his manner of cider-making. He uses wild yeasts, a term in itself that falsely implies the nature of the relationship; he does not use them, they are there regardless and he simply does not stop them from doing what they will naturally do. At times, Tom makes it sound like all he does is the labor of pressing, the rest being not down to him but to the workings of these wild yeasts.

So what are wild yeasts? Well, they are everywhere, and I genuinely do mean everywhere; they don't simply exist on the skins of unwashed apples, or in the wilder corners of our world. They live on us, on our walls, floors, and ceilings, and across everything in between. Often, at talks, Tom articulates this by holding his fist in the air, and proclaiming that "There are a million yeasts in my fist." They are invisible actors, working away at a level that is somewhat alien to us, that realm of imagination that lies beyond the naked eye.

But unlike in the world of cleaning spray adverts, such microorganisms are not always out to get us, and many of them do the most wonderful things. Ignoring the role of microbes within the human body, they give us many of our most wonderful foods and drinks, such as anything fermented—cheese, bread, cured meats, yogurt, and of course alcohol. Often their labor has been harnessed by humans to preserve food that would otherwise rot, and make raw ingredients last that much longer by changing them into a different form. It's a fascinating reflection on the workings of our world, and just how fitting for us the planet we call home is that such a process naturally occurs, one that can give us food in the sparse winter months and some of the greatest tastes and pleasures we know.

So what then are inoculated yeasts, and why are they often used in cider-making, especially if wild ones can naturally provide such benevolent things? Well, many inoculated yeasts come from wild yeasts; they are simply strains that have been isolated and grown in a laboratory. When a yeast has been isolated and cultured in a laboratory or similar artificial medium it is called a "cultured yeast." The term "inoculated" is a general term; it means the yeasts have been introduced, rather than being there naturally. Another name for this is a "pitched" yeast, also a reference to the yeast's addition, but these terms tend to be used to refer to roughly the same thing.

The purpose of such inoculated yeasts is of course control, and almost every, if not all, cider made in the mass market will use inoculated yeasts. The wild yeasts that were present in the pressed juice will usually be killed off after pressing and an inoculated yeast added instead. Otherwise variety reigns supreme, as no two populations of wild yeasts will be exactly the same or produce the same results. So the use of an inoculated yeast allows repetition, and a laboratory-precise control of the yeast strain(s) that are doing the fermentation.

But of course this does not come without its cost (in my view); the key point about wild yeasts is not that they are wild, but that they live within a complex community of many strains of wild yeasts. While more than one inoculated yeast can be added to a fermentation, fermentations with inoculated yeasts tend to see only one strain added to undertake the fermentation. Even though millions or billions of them are added, they are all the same strain, a singular replicated form, all undergoing the same actions. Wild yeasts, however, are part of an ecosystem, a vast array of genetics, of numerous strains each working in slightly different ways.

So when working with wild yeasts, a cider-maker is allowing a community of numerous different characters to ferment the cider. And while they will often do similar things, they will not by any means all have the same effect on the fermentation. The effect of this can of course be both good and bad, but it is nonetheless complex. I think of it this way: if wild yeasts are an orchestra (and one that can be open to many bad musicians…), an individual inoculated yeast is a person playing a piano (or any other single instrument); it alone can be beautiful, but even the most beautiful combination of notes cannot create the complexity of an orchestra. A piano is a complex thing in its own right, but most symphony orchestras contain a piano, and they also contain a lot of other instruments too, each unique and contributing to a greater cumulative whole.

→ Few people know the power and abundance of wild yeasts; they are everywhere.

This analogy, slightly ridiculous though it may be, highlights another point: anyone can press a key on a piano and if it's been tuned, it'll make a decent sound. It takes skill and practice to learn to play a piano well, but it takes a lot of talent to make an orchestra work. It's easier to teach an individual to play the piano well, than to train an entire ensemble for an orchestra; get a random bunch of even fairly talented musicians together and ask them to play in an orchestra and it's pretty likely to sound terrible—it needs a lot of stewardship to be made to work well. The conductor needs to know how to get the most out of these many musicians (even if it might not always look like the conductor is actually doing much, just waving their hands about), and most of the conductor's work goes on behind the scenes, before the performance gets underway, setting the stage for what is to come. They must create an environment that is conducive to their musicians' strengths and mitigates their weaknesses. The role of the cider-maker when working with wild yeasts, therefore, is more one of stewardship, their work goes on largely before the fermentation, rather than during it; they set the stage for the yeasts to do their thing. You could also think of the comparison between wild and inoculated yeasts as like the difference between a band and one individual playing one instrument (and wild yeasts really can be as varied and dependent on personal taste as different bands…), in this sense the cider world is like the world of music: you have the mass-market cider-makers

↓↘ Flor, a thin layer of yeast that sometimes gathers on top of the cider during the fermentation process.

churning out sugary-sweet manufactured pop, while the world of fine makers is creating new and differing sounds. Some like the high notes of acidity, some the deep base of Herefordshire tannins—each to their own taste.

So using an inoculated yeast holds certain certainties; it can be pitch perfect as written on the packet in which it comes. And using wild yeasts can at first or in the wrong hands (or even at times in the right hands) create a discordant cacophony, potentially a costly and high-risk thing when compared to an inoculated yeast. But get it right, know how to work with wild yeasts, and a symphony can resound.

So how do wild yeasts operate? Well, the variation of their communities is locale-specific to the cider house. A single farm, even a single room or single barrel, may contain a differently composed community. Each time a cider-maker presses and fills a container with apple juice, they are providing a nirvana for those yeasts naturally present in the ambient environment, who are able to gorge on the juice's rich sugar. Many different strains of yeast play their roles at different stages: different strains of apiculate yeasts (defined by their lemon-shaped cells) do a lot of the early work up to a few percent alcohol. After that others, such as saccharomyces strains (rod-like in shape), take over, each affecting the fermenting cider in its own way.

Because they work for varying durations, and at different (while often overlapping) stages in the fermentation, the workings of wild yeasts are very hard to measure. Even if you can measure precisely which yeasts are working on a fermentation at any one point in time, the community is ever-changing, meaning that to truly map such a fermentation you would need to be able to measure the changing yeast population in real time. This is not a thing I know much about, and yet still the complexity is baffling. When you really think on it all, of the billions of yeasts involved, it's a little like trying to comprehend all of the stars in our galaxy.

So it's a surreal and fascinating relationship, that of a cider-maker and the yeasts that do their cider-making. In the first few years of cider-making, a new cider-maker will often detect changes in their cider, compared to their cider of the previous year(s), if made from wild yeasts. This is as the community of wild yeasts in their cider house evolves, fueled by their cider making. But also, after a maker has been working for a good few years, their cider will often settle into a house style, by which I mean a certain set of taste characteristics seem to become archetypal for that cider-maker. This is, of course, mostly based on factors such as the taste, aims, and refinement of making of that maker, and their choice of apples, equipment, and method, but is also defined to a degree for them by their community of wild yeasts.

# "NATURAL CIDER"

When working with wild yeasts, a sense of locale made evident in the cider is not just down to the apple trees in the ground, or the soil they sit in; the wild yeast community of that specific locale also shapes the cider.

Here we are bordering on the world of "natural wine," both in methodology and the many questions the cider-maker has to confront. There's always a lot of debate about the definition of "natural wine," and the same is true for "natural cider." I've seen panel discussions where each of the panelists puts forward a different remit for the domain of natural cider, but I find these discussions all a little futile; there fundamentally is no objective definition, and everyone involved will never agree. The definition can be thought of more as a sliding scale or as different doctrines, being more or less extreme depending on who you ask. For me however, the most important factor in "natural cider-making" is the use of wild yeasts. It's not biodynamic farming or the use of sulfites, but the yeasts, as they are the thing that converts the juice into the alcoholic drink that results. This drink came into existence as naturally as possible, from nothing but the juice of apples, thanks to the wild yeasts awaiting, not through yeasts manipulated and added.

Another term used in the place of "natural" is "minimal intervention," which is in many ways a better term, even if lacking the marketing clout of the word "natural," and perhaps underplaying the nuance involved. It does, however, highlight the overall ethos of many makers who work with wild yeasts, that of working with what will occur naturally, not trying to overly control or negate this. It says that the maker can create the playing field, by pressing the apples and choosing the container, but they do not intervene in the game itself; its playing is left to the unbeatable complexities of a natural transformation.

Of course, intervening in the fermentation, after the fruit has been pressed, is one thing, and many elements of intervention can be avoided before this, such as the use of pesticides; or after this, such as the use of sulfites and filtration. And avoiding such interventions is often a huge part of much natural wine-making, but that is a whole other discussion, and not one I am going to go into here. A thing I'd rather highlight is that when working in this manner, with wild yeasts and minimal intervention, a

→ "Natural cider" has complexity thanks to the maker not interfering more than necessary, letting nature run its course.

cider-maker really has only three main things they can control: fruit choice (varieties, including how they were grown, where they came from, etc.), what to ferment in (such as barrel, steel tank, etc.), and time (how long to age the cider and under what conditions). They can add layers later, like making the cider sparkle, but they set out with only these three tools. With so few tools at their disposal (no additives to add, no complex scientific processes to apply), these three choices become very important for the cider-maker, and they can be very nuanced things.

Perhaps the most notable point to be made about wild yeasts and "natural cider" in general, which is also true for wine, is that at one time all ciders were "natural." Before cultured yeasts existed, fermentation just happened naturally, and with apples from orchards that had never seen pesticides, as they did not yet exist. Across most of its history, its heyday included, wild yeasts were the only option for making cider and so were the basis of its evolution. The cider-maker's ability to intervene was limited to our collective understanding, and the role of yeasts in making alcohol was not even known; it was not until the mid-19th century that yeasts were connected to fermentation, and not until the 20th that their workings were truly understood. So in the wider scheme of things, the existence of inoculated yeasts has been fairly short, and their development has tended to go hand in hand with the industrialization of cider-making.

It's also worth saying that the priorities of the fullest industrial approach to alcohol and food production can leach out quality for the consumer, in preference for other things. An example is given in Bursting Bubbles by Robert Walters, where he makes the point that all chickens were once freerange, they grew at the pace nature allowed, and their environment varied as nature did; then along came battery farming to control these factors. In came far cheaper chicken, each bird carrying far more meat, eaten more often by more people, but with facile faster-grown flesh: abundant, cheap, and lacking in flavor.

So "natural" as a way of making is not new; its present-day incarnation is more a reclaiming of natural complexity from the near all-encompassing march of the industrialization of food and drink manufacture. It's giving up some of the forms of control we have discovered, for the sake of the abundance that already came in-built. The key difference is we now understand and know how to work with this abundance far better. There are, of course, exceptions that have held firm in the prevailing winds: in Asturias for example, among other regions in northern Spain, the biggest cider-

makers still use wild yeast fermentations and have a grand history of doing so; their legendary *Sidra Natural* is perhaps the greatest example of a culture of cider-making done with truly enviable standards.

So to lay my cards on the table where yeasts in cider are concerned, I don't know that people can beat nature in this game, even with our now great scientific understanding

← The Traditional (aka 'Champagne') Method starts off with a crown cap. A mushroom cork is only added at the end, when the bottle is ready to sell.

and ability to manipulate. My personal default finds the natural world more powerful than the man-made; I am for example always more in awe of a mountain than a skyscraper. Looked at objectively, the tallest skyscraper has nothing on the scale of mountains; the Burj Khalifa is an 828-meter hollow frame of metal, concrete, and glass, Mount Everest is 8,848 meters of rock that people can still barely reach the peak of, around one in ten having died trying. But regardless, where cider-making is concerned, and by evidence of my taste buds, the best a maker can do is act as nature's greatest possible steward. To try to reach cider's peak as afforded by wild yeasts, as its peak is higher than the view from the tallest inoculated yeast tower. It's the awe of nature, we can only hope to be as complex as its working, and so working with its workings would seem to yield the greatest complexity.

You also have to remember that all things are relative, and all things have their place. Where we are thinking of cider like wine, things will be judged relative to wine. Cider only tends to be around half the alcohol level of wine, and higher alcohol levels tend to give greater levels of complexity (as a very loose rule). So to live up to this relative, and to surpass expectations, the workings of a wild fermentation can be a cider's doorway to complexity.

In spite of all I've just said, inoculated yeasts can produce exquisite cider; the clean softness or singular profile that such a yeast can often create in a cider can be wonderful. A maker can also ferment a number of different batches of cider, each with different inoculated yeasts, and then blend these different results, going some way to replicating the variety of wild yeasts but in a more controlled manner. There are also situations in which a maker has to use an inoculated yeast. For example, ice cider-making can require it, or a Traditional Method (same as Champagne Method; see page 148) cider uses an inoculated yeast for a second fermentation in the bottle. And while the debate about the idea of a "natural" approach meanders on, it's worth remembering the counterpoint that it is easy to cast a naive nostalgic eye over the past, without remembering just how bad most wines and ciders would have been a few hundred years ago by today's standards, and just how far so much of the making of alcohol has come, largely thanks to such scientific understanding.

What other differences exist between wild and inoculated yeasts, beyond opinion? I'd add that the use of wild yeasts tends to require more time to ferment than that of purposefully virile cultured yeasts. Some inoculated yeasts used in mass-market making can ferment juice (or concentrate) into "cider" in just a few weeks. In contrast to this, even in speed-giving warmer temperatures, a wild yeast fermentation will usually take a matter of months.

# WHAT TO NURTURE IT IN

The choice of container a cider is actually fermented in is a fun one; there truly is no right answer, and the array of different vessels or containers adds yet another layer of variety to the world of finest ciders. Some have their historic charms, being exquisite creations in their own rights, such as the many different kinds of wooden barrel that can be used. For those makers who want only the fruit to speak and not the vessel, the contemporary crispness of stainless-steel tanks can be the answer.

As with so many of the choices the cider-maker has to make, it all comes back to personal preference and the aims of that cider-maker. A new maker will have to confront these choices and work out their answers as they go. Many established makers may use a mix of vessels, to make the most of the variety they provide. Brand-new barrels, for example, can have a very potent effect on a cider, but blend such a cider with a cider from a steel tank or a barrel that has been used for cider-making a few times already and the effect will be tempered by the blend.

I say "nurture" in this segment's title, rather than just "ferment" in, as the choice of vessel will affect the cider not just during fermentation, but also as it matures after fermentation. So let's begin with barrels, the grand old champions of nurturing fine liquor. Through marketing many of us know the smooth and mellowing effect that barrels can have, bringing to mind the idea of vanilla and similar smooth tones. The effects of barrels in cider, loosely speaking, are similar to other alcohols such as wine: softening tannins, darkening tones, and likely imparting some flavor from the timber. Maturing a cider in a barrel can have a substantial effect, and supposedly it is during maturing that the barrel's effect is most greatly imparted to the cider, more so than during the fermentation.

The barrels used can be new or old. New barrels can be pretty domineering for cider, so former-use barrels are often favored; they also hold varied characteristics thanks to their previous use, and are also far less expensive than new barrels. There are many possibilities when it comes to former-use barrels, the spectrum being as broad as are barrels' uses: Tom Oliver, for example, has many kinds, such as old wine, whisky, and rum barrels. An old Bourbon whiskey barrel (Bourbon barrels are toasted), for example, seemed to impart a near dried-coconut element to the taste of a cider made down at Starvecrow, in Sussex in England (see page 147). And the guys at Little Pomona Cidery in Herefordshire (see page 143) used a former Moscatel wine barrel for one of their blends. Ryan Burk at Angry Orchard Walden in New York State (see page 117) has a collection of former Calvados barrels; there's something poetic and seemingly full circle about using barrels that once contained cider brandy to make cider.

Another container commonly used is the stainless-steel tank. For those makers who want "nothing but the fruit to speak," such as James Marsden at Gregg's Pit in Herefordshire, stainless steel is the best choice. One of the main differences between all of the types of containers that can be used is to do with the "micro-oxygenation" (a gradual exposure to air, enough to have certain desired effects on the cider, but not enough to spoil it). A barrel is perhaps the prime example of a container that allows such micro-oxygenation. This also means it gives off what is called the "angels' share" (a portion of the liquid that evaporates away through the barrel into the air—a gift to the angels!). A stainless-steel tank, however, is highly restrictive of this. "Inertness" is another factor (a vessel that is inert is effectively "flavorless"). Stainless steel is inert, whereas a barrel will have numerous effects; micro-oxygenation and interaction with microflora within the wood, for example, will all alter the cider's flavor.

One of the joys of barrels is that they are usually relatively small, so a maker will get more batches and thus more variation from the same volume of cider. This can be useful for blending, but also to limit the risk from a bad batch. The same can be true of stainless-steel tanks, and many of the best small-batch makers use many small stainless-

→ Old meets new with steel tanks sat alongside wooden barrels at Find & Foster in Devon.

steel tanks or similar to get a similar level of variety. Stainless-steel tanks can also be huge and are the prevailing choice of mass-market makers.

Other options for the materials that vessels can be made from include plastic, glass, concrete, terracotta; and new or other kinds of container are being invented or adopted from other walks in the world of alcohol all the time. Ben Walgate of Starvecrow Cider and Tillingham Wines, for example, is one of the few makers in the UK using qvevri to ferment some of his ciders; qvevri are large clay amphorae, made of terracotta, that are buried in the ground and have been used in wine-making in Georgia for thousands of years. They also allow a level of micro-oxygenation, and their distinctive form collects the lees at the base of the vessel. The results of his wild yeast fermentations in them have been fascinating. With his un-tannic varieties creating ciders with a texture similar to tannins on the tail. It's a slight chalkiness, perhaps coming from the lees (see page 139) or flor within the qvevri, or from the qvevri itself, I really don't know.

## SECONDARY MALOLACTIC "FERMENTATION"

When nurturing a cider, when given enough time and under the right conditions, a secondary malolactic "fermentation" can take place. I say "fermentation" in inverted commas as it isn't technically a fermentation at all, as bacteria rather than yeast are what make it happen. The key to it is that malic acid (the archetypal apple acid taste) is converted to lactic acid, which tastes notably less acidic. So the cider is mellowed on the palate, and sharper becomes smoother, often with a creamier texture and even a slight buttery taste. A secondary malolactic fermentation can be induced artificially, but in the right circumstances will happen naturally if allowed to.

# THE ROLE OF THE BOTTLE

Nurturing does not stop at the barrel or tank stage—the bottle also plays a role. Not during the whole fermentation (as even a Champagne bottle cannot take the pressure a full fermentation will create), but in the late stages, or after fermentation, the bottle can become the vessel. Cider will continue developing in the weeks, months, and years after it has been put in a bottle, and the bottle alone is not some kind of stop button, with the cider staying exactly one way until it "goes off." Many ciders are stabilized when they are put into bottles, and there are a number of ways to do so, but even with these a cider will keep changing to some degree. So the life cycle of a cider, even in its less active later stages, is still an ever-changing and evolving thing.

When a naturally sparkling cider is being made a sediment will form. This sediment, called the "lees," is the dead or residual yeasts falling to the bottom of the bottle, having done their job. But lees exist throughout any fermentation, and not just in the bottle. Whether from a wild or inoculated yeast fermentation, they are produced in abundance and sink down to form a thick layer at the bottom of the barrel or tank; think of them like sediment in the bottom of a bottle, but on a far more substantial scale. They look a little like a fine dust or sand that has been mixed into water, and are known as the "gross lees." As lees also occur in the bottle, when a naturally sparkling cider is being made, they affect the taste of the cider. How long the cider is left to age on the lees in the bottle dictates how much of an effect the lees have on the taste. A process called autolysis occurs, as enzymes break down the yeast cells, often imparting a certain biscuity, toasty, or nutty element to the taste of the cider.

Over time, different ciders will behave differently in the bottle, and not all will age in the same way. Often a cider will lose any fresher, fruitier characteristics it may have after enough time, and the cider will fade somewhat (in my experience, this will be particularly fast or pronounced in a cider that has had a lot of manipulation and intervention during its making, and such bottles can fade very notably). This often happens over a period of two or three years, after which the cider will taste less youthful and vibrant, and in its place a more mature taste will develop. Things like tannins can then taste far more prominent. But this is not always the case, while some ciders suffer from this change, others suit it well, or even improve notably with aging beyond this time frame.

Overall, the aging of cider is a subject that needs more understanding. I keep an archive of up to a dozen bottles of every batch of cider and perry that we sell (it's starting to fill up rather a lot of space!), in order to taste how they age and see what changes occur year on year.

Many of the finest makers operating today work across a timeframe from around six months up to five or so years, with the average aging being around two years or more for ciders that develop well with time. Historically, there is little to go on, as the industrialization of cider over the past century has really mitigated the role of aging in cider-making. But there are fascinating snippets from the past that can be found in literature. In his wonderful book *The History of Virtues of Cyder*, for example, Roger French references that following the adoption of bottling the aging of ciders increased in timespan: in the 18th century seven years' aging is noted, and by the 19th century as long as 20 to 30 years.

→ Bottles resting on a *pupitre*, a rack used as part of the "Champagne Method."

# SWEET OR DRY?

Sweetness is, of course, a spectrum, ranging from *Dry* (no sugar) at one end, through *Medium Dry*, *Medium*, and *Medium Sweet*, to *Sweet* at the other. But a really important fact to know is that cider is not by default naturally sweet, although the creations of the mass market may have given many people the impression that it is. There is no such thing as an apple variety that simply stays sweet when fully fermented (very minor exceptions can apply under certain circumstances, such as from a thing called "watercore" which can occur in adverse environmental conditions). Perry pears can ferment fully but still retain sweetness, owing to an unfermentable sugar called *sorbitol*. The reality is that left to their own devices, wild or inoculated yeasts will ferment any cider to dry, unless something goes wrong along the way to halt the fermentation, or steps are taken by the cider-maker to stop the cider fermenting fully.

The most common method for making a cider not dry is adding something sweet after the fermentation. I say most common because this is how it's often done in the mass market, and also at smaller scales. Artificial sweeteners are often used, or natural sugars, to get the desired level of sweetness. It's called backsweetening, and it can also be done with unfermented apple juice, so that the natural sugars in the juice are the thing adding the sweetness. But there are also a number of ways that a maker can stop the yeasts fermenting the cider to dry. Some of the interventions that can be used to do this require complex technical machinery, while others are fairly simple.

Those makers with the greatest aspiration however, wishing to make a cider that is not totally dry in the most refined manner, will use a method called Keeving (see page 154) or will make Ice Cider (an exquisite dessert wine-like drink; see page 158). Both of them constitute styles in their own right, so let's get stuck into all of the styles that fine cider can hold.

# CIDER STYLES

## STILL

*Key element:*    The cider is not sparkling (but it also does not have extra/other layers of technique applied, such as those that make an Ice Cider or a Hybrid Cider; it is unsparkling cider, pure and simple).

*Example:*    Little Pomona, Old Man & the Bee 2016

What is still cider? Put very simply, still cider is cider that is not sparkling. And just as still wine dominates the world of wine, being the most abundant thing on one hand and the greatest expression of terrior/locale on the other, so too can you look at still cider as the purest expression of a cider, and the place from which it came.

Still cider is a surreal thing. Seemingly the simplest of cider styles, this unassuming form, lacking the additions of method of many ciders, is in fact the most nuanced and most varied of any style. This is as it is cider laid bare; there are no bubbles nor layers of technique for any faults to hide behind, making it cider pure and simple. But it requires skill to work in this "less is more" manner—a maker has to really get the most out of their chosen fruit, and be sure to guide their fermentations to a good result.

Without layers added atop, when it is left alone and untampered with, this is cider as nature intended, and as a result an expression of the fruit and the locale of its growing can be more evident than in perhaps any other style. I am, of course, referring to still cider in its finest form here, at its highest ideal, as not all (or in some cases any of these assertions) hold true for all still ciders. Just as still cider's nuanced depths can hold so much potential, so too can it be the domain of rough stuff, the classic category of scrumpy at its worst.

I am often surprised when members of the public tell me, and it happens surprisingly often, that they didn't know still cider was a thing, or even existed. Such is the tempo toned by the bubbles of the mass market. But just as no cider will be naturally sweet without the hand of man (or happy accident), no cider will be sparkling unless the maker makes it so. We'll go into how makers make cider sparkle in more detail in the subsections: Pet Nat (see page 145) and Traditional Method (see page 148) as there are a number of ways.

In the world of wine, it is still wines that dominate; think of wine, and you're likely thinking of a still red or white. Still takes much less technical effort than sparkling, but it can be rich in quality and depth. And as with still wine, still cider has huge variety built in. The character of a single-apple variety can really stand out in a still cider, making for an incredibly broad spectrum of possibilities. The spectrum of sparkling ciders is in many ways less pronounced as the gas that makes a cider sparkling, as well as the byproducts of the process (sediment), affect the flavor of the cider, giving them a point of commonality not found in still cider.

The most complex still fine ciders will be dry (with the exception of Ice Cider; see pages 158–161), having fermented the fullest and allowing the greatest complexity to develop in the process. But many of my favorite still ciders have been aged substantially after fermentation, particularly with some time in barrel, where micro-oxygenation seems to mellow the cider in wonderful ways. An overly robust cider can become incredibly nuanced, when given enough time in this way. And a secondary malolactic "fermentation" (see page 138) can also drop the acidity tasted on the palate, mellowing the cider further.

• MAKERS: **JAMES AND SUSANNA FORBES, LITTLE POMONA CIDERY, HEREFORDSHIRE**

Little Pomona is run by James and Susanna Forbes—delightful people, making fascinating cider. They both have a background in the world of alcohol, the influences of which steer them as they make cider in Herefordshire, having moved there to buy an orchard a number of years ago. Wine-world thoughts in particular come into play, and their "house style" has a higher level of acidity than many more traditional cider-makers would produce. But unlike some cider-makers who stem from wine, they do not try to force the ways of wine wholesale onto cider. Often when this is the case, the cider that results will

be too constrained and muted; the ways of wine may work well for alcohol levels of 10% plus, but at the lower alcohols of cider they can create something a little too plain. What is needed, as these guys know, is the right mix, taking reference from both the world of wine and the world of traditional cider.

The 2016 season's blend of Old Man & the Bee (named after the farmer who planted the orchard and the bees that pollinate the fruit) combined: Harry Masters Jersey (75%), Dabinett (11%), Foxwhelp (9%), and Ellis Bitter (5%). For me, this blend of four varieties gives an extra bit of complexity, that extra layer than a blend of just two or three might. All of the fruit came from 20-year-old standard trees in their own orchard, which is south-south-west facing, and sat on a gentle slope made up of red clay soils. The Foxwhelp in the blend was barrel-aged in former whisky barrels, for over two years. The remaining varieties in the blend were fermented in tank, all with wild yeasts, and the cider as a whole underwent a secondary malolactic fermentation.

This is a robust, full-bodied, bone-dry cider. It is high in acid and high in tannins. It is a world away from the ciders of the mass market. The Foxwhelp component, even though only a small percentage of the blend, increases the acidity, lending a more vibrant citrus element to the cider. The nose has a fascinating combination of fruitiness and savoriness, with that slightly meaty nose of Dabinett, and slight butteriness from fruit. It's got the subtle depths of dried old timber, being rich but mellow. And it really opens up in the mouth, rising in richness as it's tasted. With a bit of dried apricot and a slightly more oxidized note; a sherry-like, higher alcohol element. Then at the tail a more bitter element from the tannins kicks in, tasting slightly slate-like in its bitterness.

# PET NAT

*Also known as:*   Pétillant Naturel (translation from French: naturally
                   sparkling), Ancestral Method, Rural Method

*Key element:*     The key to this style is that the cider is naturally sparkling
                   (without sugar or yeast having been added) and there is
                   a sediment in the bottle.

*Example:*         Starvecrow Pet Nat 2018

To set the scene, let's look a little at the difference between naturally and artificially sparkling (carbonated) drinks. When a drink is carbonated, gas is added to the cider artificially, by being forced to dissolve in the liquid under high pressure. William Brownrigg, a doctor from Cumberland in the north of England, was supposedly the first person to artificially carbonate water, doing so in the 1740s. Large-scale carbonation of water began in 1781, with a certain J. J. Schweppe founding Schweppes in Switzerland in 1783.

Naturally sparkling drinks were, of course, discovered before carbonation, with carbonation aiming to synthesize this natural effect. So how do you make a drink naturally sparkling? The key is fermentation, as carbon dioxide is released during a fermentation. When carbon dioxide is not allowed to leave the bottle, it is forced to dissolve in the liquid as the pressure builds up. As carbon dioxide is only weakly soluble in water, when a bottle is opened and the liquid comes into contact with normal atmospheric pressure, it forms bubbles as the gas is released.

In the early stages of fermentation, such as in a barrel or tank, an air lock will be fitted to the top of the vessel to allow these gases to escape, while also allowing no air to get in. The key to all naturally sparkling drinks, as opposed to carbonated drinks, is that the carbon dioxide that makes the drink sparkle has come from fermentation.

In many ways, Pet Nat is the simplest form of naturally sparkling cider, as it takes less labor from the maker than other naturally sparkling methods, and so prices for it tend to be cheaper. It likely makes sense then, to learn that the oldest known sparkling wine was made with this method. The oldest written recording describes the sale of sparkling wine in glass flasks sealed by cork, at the Abbaye de Saint-Hilaire in Limoux, southern France. The area is also not far from the border with Spain, and so had easy access to Catalan cork forests.

But there is a cost, or can be, to this simplicity for the maker. Pet Nat can be a fairly risky way of making a cider sparkle, and ciders made with this method can vary hugely in their level of sparkle; even the best maker can never be 100 percent certain exactly how sparkling a Pet Nat cider will end up being. The cider can turn out barely sparkling, or even become so sparkling that it can burst a bottle or pop its own cork. This is because while a maker can measure the amount of sugar in the still fermenting cider before they put it in the bottle, and to a very decent accuracy, they cannot know exactly when the cider will stop fermenting. The amount of sugar in the juice in each bottle can also vary. So it may stop fermenting slightly before it becomes fully dry, and if it does there will be fewer bubbles. If, however, it ferments further than they expect, the cider may be more sparkling than they desired; even gushing from the bottle when opened.

How lightly or vigorously bubbly a cider is, is based simply on the amount of gas dissolved in the liquid. So for naturally sparkling ciders, how bubbly they are is based simply on how much fermentation has happened in the bottle, and for Pet Nat ciders, this can really vary.

Other factors can also play their part, for example when the cider is bottled; if it is bottled in different batches across different days, not all of the cider will be going into bottle in exactly the same state or under the same conditions. Such that some say it's best to bottle Pet Nat ciders when there's high atmospheric pressure, as you retain the most carbon dioxide dissolved in the liquid. Some also say the phases of the moon play a part; that's how variable Pet Nat can be!

But it's not just the amount of bubbles that can vary: as the amount of fermentation that happens in the bottle will vary, so too will the amount of sediment. And this sediment will affect the taste and texture of the cider, as already mentioned, through the breakdown (autolysis) of the yeast cells that make up the sediment.

A good Pet Nat cider will be neither overly nor underly sparkling, with either a wonderful creamy or lively texture. The sediment will add a nice variability to the texture of the cider, without being too pronounced (if there's a sandstorm in the bottom of the bottle, it will dominate the cider, and give it a somewhat powdery texture, unless left to settle and carefully poured).

As Pet Nat ciders are put in bottle before the cider has finished fermenting, they tend to be ready before most other styles. As soon as the fermentation has finished, it's ready to drink and so it might be ready after only six or nine months. This means Pet Nat can make for a vibrant, youthful cider. And as such, many working in this way favor the fresh, juicy, full fruit taste that can come with this youth. So it's often said that Pet Nat ciders don't age that well, but I do know of some wonderful exceptions to this.

• MAKERS: **BEN WALGATE AND STEVE REEVE, STARVECROW CIDER, SUSSEX**

Ben Walgate is first and foremost a wine-maker, making some exceptional natural wines near Rye in East Sussex. Moving to this part of England to set up his own winery, Tillingham Wines, is what set him down a path of making cider in ways often reserved for wine. His experiments with qvevri for fermenting, and methods such as Pet Nat, have created fascinating things from non-traditional cider apple varieties. His co-founder of Starvecrow, Steve Reeve, has the orchards, and his family have farmed on the site for generations.

The orchards sit on Wadhurst clay over sandstone, close to the sea, at an altitude of around 100 feet (30 meters) above sea level, with glimpses of water shimmering away in the distance visible from the orchards. The trees themselves can be up to 60 years of age.

In the blend are Bramley, Golden, Charles Ross, and Braeburn apples. Pet Nat can be great with this kind of fruit and a wild yeast fermentation, as is the case here; this bottle has a lovely mix of acidity and full fruit flavor, all with the sharpness and minerality of the vibrant bubbles.

This cider is crisp and sharp. There's something floral on the nose with a hint of honey, and a lively sparkle in the mouth, bouncing on the tongue like popping candy. The taste has straw, and the sharpness of gooseberry, being both fruity and a bit tart. The texture is fascinating, with the sediment from the fermentation in the bottle giving the cider a light haze, and a slightly clay-like taste on the end of the palate. It's mineral side is a little like granite, rich in ores.

# TRADITIONAL METHOD

*Also known as:*   Methode Champenoise (Champagne Method), Bottle
Fermented, Bottle Conditioning (can also refer to a single
fermentation completed in the bottle, similar to Pet Nat,
see page 145)

*Key element:*   A whole other fermentation (called a secondary
fermentation) is made to happen inside the bottle, to give
a vigorous natural sparkle. This second fermentation tends
to give a naturally sparkling cider that is higher in alcohol
than Pet Nat ciders.

*Example:*   Methode Traditionelle Find & Foster

If Pet Nat is sometimes said to be the "quick and dirty" approach to creating
a naturally sparkling drink, then this is the "slow and clean" approach (except
perhaps for the disgorging part, explained shortly). This method is far more
controlled, as instead of bottling the cider while still fermenting, the maker
lets it fully ferment and then creates a second fermentation in the bottle. As
the maker has created the fermentation, by adding sugar and yeast, the extent
of the fermentation is far more consistent and predictable, meaning so too
is the level of bubbles that result in the bottle. And each separate bottle
within the same batch will have more or less the same level of sparkle. In
French, this addition of sugar and yeast is known as the *liqueur de tirage*, and
it is usually added with a small amount of cider so that it is in solution.

The key to this method is the secondary fermentation that happens in the
bottle. And what marks it out as a style, as opposed to Pet Nat, is that the
yeast and sugar have been added, one of the knock-on effects of which is to
create a higher level of alcohol, as two fermentations have occurred, rather
than the single fermentation of Pet Nat. This means Traditional Method
ciders often reach alcohol levels of around 8% abv, gaining the extra
complexity these higher alcohols can lend in the process.

This technique can be particularly fitting for using with East Coast fruit
(see page 70), as the lower levels of tannic complexity of such fruit can be
compensated for by this higher alcohol complexity, and as the acidity that
dominates its palate can work well with bubbles, as it does in sparkling white
wine, giving crispness and vibrancy. Higher acid levels also help such a cider
age well, which can be an important part of the method.

Aging is often associated with the Traditional Method, and the most famous version of this method comes from the world of wine: the Champagne Method. It is the full method, if you will, combining almost all of the components we are about to speak about. Most often, ciders made in this manner are given at least a year and a half to mature in the bottle, on the lees, before being sold. This timespan allows acidity to mellow, as well as allowing autolysis of the yeast cells in the lees, which give an extra element of complexity to the drink. Aging, in Champagne, legally requires the wine to be aged for at least 15 months in the bottle, at least 12 of which must be on the lees. And for vintage Champagne, the minimum aging time allowed is three years, but can be as long as eight or even ten years.

Once the cider has been aged on the lees, there are two possible routes for the cider-maker to go down: disgorged or un-disgorged. Basically this means "removing the lees" or "leaving the lees." The purpose of disgorging is to make the drink naturally sparkling but crystal clear and free of any sediment, for when it is sold. When a drink is un-disgorged, the sediment of course stays in the bottle.

The full Traditional Method is disgorged, which is also the way of the Methode Champenoise. While only a wine can be called Champagne, and only when made in a legally defined manner and within the Champagne Region of France, pretty much the exact same technique is often used in cider-making. So let's run through how disgorging works, as removing the lees from the bottle is no simple task (considering the bottle is sealed and contains as much pressure as it does; but it is this very pressure that is used for the process of disgorging).

Many might assume Champagne is made with the mushroom cork it has when it is sold, but it doesn't. The mushroom cork is not added until after the drink has finished its secondary fermentation, has been disgorged, and is ready to sell, so at the last minute. Until this point it has a crown cap. The reason why is that this crown cap is removed and discarded when the bottle is disgorged, and it would be wasteful to remove and throw away a mushroom cork in this way. The crown caps are also especially adapted for the job of riddling, a process that occurs before the disgorging. The aim of riddling is to get all of the lees to collect and clump together in the neck of the bottle, against the crown cap. To do so, the bottle is turned upside down, to an angle of around 45 degrees, and over a period of four to six weeks, the bottle is turned a quarter turn a few times a day, by hand. At the end of the cycle, with these many small turns, even the finest particles of sediment should now hopefully have sunk down to the neck of the bottle and be clumped together. This riddling process is usually done on a special A-frame rack, called a pupitre or riddling rack. Historically, this process has also been done in other ways, such as with a box of sand, and the legend goes that a kitchen table with holes drilled in it formed the first ever pupitre.

There are now, of course, machines that can do this, and they are used widely across the Champagne region for its sparkling wine, which are quicker than doing it by hand. They are not the cheapest piece of equipment for a small cider-maker, so many cider-makers still do this by hand. It is also certainly more charming to see, when done by hand on these racks, than in the steel cage of an automated machine, and some of the most prestigious Champagnes are still riddled by hand. Often the bottles are marked on their bases with a white line, so the maker can keep track easily of what has and has not been turned. It's also good to give the bottle a slight knock against the wooden rack when turning, to help loosen the fine sediment in the bottle from the glass, and encourage it to sink down to the neck of the bottle.

After the sediment has been slowly collected in the neck of the upturned bottle comes the disgorging. Basically, disgorging is opening these bottles, so the pressure of the sparkling drink within pushes the sediment in the neck out of the bottle, leaving you without any sediment in the bottle. But of course it is a little more fiddly than that, and takes a lot of practice to do well. Firstly, this means both removing all of the sediment, but losing as little of the drink as possible. To do this, you begin with the neck still pointed downward, and pop the crown cap while turning the bottle upright as the bubble in the bottle rises to the neck, then slide your thumb over the open mouth of the bottle, to stop the bubbling cider escaping.

To make this process easier, the necks, and only the necks, of the bottles are often frozen, so the clumped-together sediment gets locked into a plug of ice. This means when the bottle is opened, a clean plug of ice pops out, taking all the sediment with it. A cold cider will also keep more dissolved carbon dioxide, meaning you lose less cider (anyone who has opened a warm sparkling wine will know how much more vigorous it is). But you don't have to use this freezing method, and when disgorging is done without freezing it is described as *à la volée*, French for "on the fly." It takes skill, and even then it can be a messy process.

Some of the cider is inevitably lost in the process, and so it is topped up from another bottle, before the mushroom cork is applied. If this is all you do, the cider will be Brut, meaning dry. So in many cases, a maker will add what is called a dosage (also known as the *liqueur d'expedition* in French): a chosen amount of sugar, usually mixed with a small amount of the cider, that gives the finished cider the desired amount of sweetness. This is known as residual sweetness, as is any sweetness that remains in a cider which is ready to sell. Once the mushroom cork goes in the bottle, it's ready to sell.

So as you can likely now tell, following the many paragraphs you've just read, this is quite a technical technique! And so it has its substantial costs in terms of labor, which of course substantially increases the price of the cider. Risky though Pet Nat can be, it is significantly cheaper for the maker to do as a method.

Technically, the term "Traditional Method" is used to describe the full whack; riddling and disgorging, akin to the Champagne Method, rather than drinks made with a secondary fermentation that are not disgorged. But I have decided to define it in this manner, as disgorged or un-disgorged, as in my view the key thing that marks this style out is the secondary fermentation in the bottle, not the disgorging. The disgorging is mostly done for aesthetic reasons; to make the drink pristine and free of any clouding sediment. And whether a cider made in this method is disgorged or not, it has still had a secondary fermentation, as well as time aging on its lees. Not disgorging will affect the texture of the cider, and if you leave a cider that is un-disgorged to age for a decent amount of time, it will of course become more and more different to its disgorged cousin, after the same amount of time, as the lees will affect it as it ages.

Another thing to note is that the yeast added to create the secondary fermentation can be wild (taken like a sample from a live wild fermentation), as well as the usually used cultured yeast option. Cultured yeast is considered most reliable, and so many good makers will use a wild yeast fermentation for the primary fermentation, and then a cultured

→ The disgorging process, used to remove lees, or spent yeast from the bottle, resulting in a clear liquid.

yeast for the secondary fermentation in bottle, to get the best of both worlds. If a maker also has a wild yeast fermentation that is still active, they can sometimes simply add sugar, and no yeast, to fuel the fermentation to continue in the bottle, but this can still have some of the uncertainty of Pet Nat. Some makers, wanting to be as natural as possible, may even add only apple juice (as it contains sugar) to fuel the fermentation further.

A good Traditional Method cider should have a dense mousse of bubbles, but without gushing too vigorously from the bottle when opened. It should be vibrant and lively in your mouth, reminiscent of the bubbles of Champagne and other sparkling wines. I do find that there is a real art to doing this method well in cider, and a lot of it comes down to choices; it can be very easy to use only cultured yeasts and less tannic apples, and create something that is surprisingly monotone, mostly just a hit of acid and a ton of bubbles, rather than something more complex. The key lies in aging and a clever selection of varieties, to give nuance and complexity to the finished cider. It can be expensive, but done well it can be glorious. And as you'll remember from Chapter 2, making cider sparkling via a fermentation in the bottle has been done for a long time, since before the likes of Champagne were even invented. So what you are drinking when you drink a Traditional Method cider is centuries in the making, a refinement of technique that has few rivals.

• MAKERS: **POLLY AND MAT HILTON, FIND & FOSTER FINE CIDERS, DEVON**

I've already spoken of the finding and fostering that Polly and her husband Mat do; the conservation and caring for old orchards in the countryside around their home in Devon. Their approach truly connects the past with the present in cider in a fascinating way; some 90 percent of the traditional orchards of Devon have been lost since World War Two. Year after year the fruit of those few orchards that remain had been left to rot on the ground, and then along came Polly. Taking reference from travels and learning lessons from wine, her cider is complex in all ways: the techniques she uses, the many varieties she has at her fingertips, the many disparate orchards she maintains, and of course in the depths of flavor that each of her bottles holds.

This Traditional Method cider has some 27 apple varieties in its blend, most of them unknown varieties, but some they have identified, such as Ben's Red and Veitche's Perfection. To keep this cider fresh and crisp, Polly uses local cooking and eating varieties, on the East Coast end of the spectrum.

They come from orchards in the Exe Valley, from trees averaging around 90–100 years old, sat on red Devon soil.

The cider has a bright brass color, having been riddled and disgorged by hand, following a primary fermentation with wild yeasts, and a secondary with an inoculated Champagne yeast. The taste has a distinct minerally element, a slight raisin sweetness, and a notably grapey flavor. There is a slight note of leathery richness, and the smallest bit of rhubarb acidity, as well as something smoky. For me, it has a perfect level of residual sugar, so its taste eases its way from the slightest hint of sweetness, to acidity, to bitterness. Rolled around in your mouth, it gives off a steady flow of bubbles, and then a little dusting of tannins at the end. And underlying it all is that same heady pleasure, that top-of-the-brain tipsiness, that Champagne provides.

# KEEVED

*Also known as:* Normandy Method

*Key element:* The cider has been keeved, a process that stops a cider fully fermenting to dry, such that it retains some of the natural fruit sugars from the juice.

*Example:* Pilton Tamoshanta, 2016

Keeving is a unique method, one not found in wine-making, and it can make a most sumptuous cider full of complex natural sweetness. Keeving is the old English name, and it is also known as the Normandy Method, being practiced more in this part of France than in any other region in the world.

By its very nature, keeving will make a cider that is lower in alcohol than most; sometimes as low as 2%, but usually from around 3.5% up to 6.5%. This is as, described at its simplest, keeving is a process that sets a cider up to naturally stop itself fermenting before it becomes fully dry, leaving behind some of the sweetness from the juice. As it stops fermenting early, it does not create as much alcohol as it otherwise would.

This is why it is so wondrous; you are not besmirching the sanctity of the apple by adding in any number of alien sugars—a dangerous path in itself, as once you open the door to added sweetness, the scale runs right through to the most artificial of sweeteners—instead you are creating both alcohol and sweetness from the very same source. Both come from one origin, the juice itself.

How sweet the resulting cider will be depends on the extent to which it has been keeved; a more substantive keeve will leave you with more residual sugar, a less substantive keeve will lean toward the drier end of the spectrum. While the simplest way to think of it is that keeved ciders have intentionally been set up to stop fermenting early, the reality is less simple: fermentation is a powerful natural process, and willing it to stop is not an easy task.

Keeving is an old technique, yet it is a complex and technical thing to do well; it is a many layered process, requiring good knowledge of what apple varieties to use and a close eye on what unfolds. It is a precise process, naturally vulnerable to failure from inexperienced stewardship and overly warm weather. Makers set different levels, but the ambient temperature for keeving needs to be below 50–54ºF (10–12ºC), otherwise the fermentation can become too vigorous for the method to work properly. And when not done well, it holds a high risk of reductive (sulfurous, eggy) notes on the nose of the cider.

The earliest reference to keeving that I have come across is from the 1660s; although the process can occur naturally in what is called a spontaneous keeve, given the right fruit and conditions, so it would also have occurred naturally before this time. But it is also pointed out by the historian that in the 1660s those using the method did not quite fully understand how the process worked. In Hugh Stafford's *Treatise* of 1753, the writer described the means of making fine ciders "fit for a gentleman," instructing that the first pressing should be strained straight into a vessel or "keeve" and then left until a cap of pulp had started to form. It should then be drawn off via a tap about 4 in (10cm) from the bottom, into closed casks leaving both the cap and lees behind. It must be repeatedly racked thereafter "until the cyder is as sweet as you desire and ceases hissing." The resulting drink would be "soft and mellow and perfectly sweet."

Traditionally salt and chalk, or even wood ash, were added to the raw pressed juice to help precipitate a keeve. Items seemingly so specific that the discovery of this method is intriguing to imagine (presumably a happy accident…). Since these times, keeving has become better understood and actively encouraged. This is how it's done.

After the juices have been pressed from the apple, the maker will add an enzyme, one that is also naturally present in the fruit juice, and a small quantity of calcium chloride (I have also heard of someone using table salt). The result of this is that a thickened gelatinous layer forms atop the surface of the juice. It binds within it much of the protein from the juice, absorbing nitrogen and vitamins that would otherwise provide nutrients for the yeasts.

The English term for this layer atop the juice is the flying lees, and the French term it *Le Chapeau Brun* (the brown hat). It is pectin gel that forms this gelatinous layer, as it flocculates (clumps together) and is caused to rise and compact above the liquid by the start of the fermentation; a thing called the first incipient fermentation.

If the fermentation does become too vigorous, or is left too long before racking off, it can break up

→ The flying lees, or *Le Chapeau Brun* (the brown hat) is a gelatinous layer that forms on the cider.

the flying lees, seeing them fall back into the juice below, stopping the cider being clear and reintroducing some of the nutrients to the juice. But if timed well and done at the right temperature, a clear, slow-fermenting, low-nutrient juice can be gently tapped off (called racking) from beneath the flying lees, leaving the lees—both flying and bottom-bound—behind.

As this juice ferments, being depleted in nutrients (that are needed by the yeast for fermentation) and with carbon dioxide and alcohol building up in the liquid, the fermentation will eventually cease as the yeasts give up, and a cider will result that holds a natural residual sweetness. When bottled in the latter throes of fermentation, before the yeasts give up, a duration of as little as four weeks will produce a beautiful, fine natural sparkle in the bottle. The cider will be effervescent in feel and will emanate a deep, oxidized amber color.

In theory, once the yeasts have given up and the fermentation ceases, you could bottle the cider and sell it as still. But keeved ciders are almost always sparkling. There are two reasons for this, one of quality, one of caution. Firstly, the process of Pet Nat combines with keeved cider to glorious effect (I categorize them as two separate styles, even though the Pet Nat method is usually applied to keeved ciders, as keeved ciders are so unique).

The other reason is because there is still residual sugar in the cider, meaning there is still the potential that it could start fermenting again. The fermentation could simply have been slowed or have gone dormant in cold temperatures. Imagine labeling hundreds of bottle as "still," only to find the bottled cider starts refermenting and as such makes itself sparkling! Refermentation can also be the stuff of greater worry, posing a threat to the bottle itself. If the bottle is not strong enough and the refermentation too strong, the pressure can break the bottle or the seal.

You could also say that keeved cider is a little like the Beaujolais Nouveau of the cider world, as it is usually among the first cider to be ready in the season (owing to the shorter fermentation). It is very juicy and full in fruit, and it tends to be best drunk when young, when its youthful characteristics are at full flight. Although, that said, it can age well sometimes, particularly the more tannic keeved cider, such as some of the wonderful keeved bottles that Tom Oliver makes.

I find that the best keeved ciders tend to be slightly higher in tannins than most, as the traditional cider apples that provide these tannins give complexity to the cider, even at the lower alcohols that keeving usually creates. Another thing that marks out keeved cider is that the apples used cannot be too acidic; keeving simply will not work if the juice is too high in acid. This means keeved ciders are low in acidity, and it is incredibly hard to keeve with East Coast fruit, for example.

Keeved cider at its best should be sumptuous in its complex natural sugars. The sweetness should not be monotone and should evolve and develop as it is tasted. It should not be simply juicy, or juice-like. Keeved ciders tend to have a softer, more rounded form on the palate than most, but this softness can be glorious, making for an easy-drinking, accessible cider that can be drunk with lunch (the low alcohol helps too). It should be full of youthful fruit flavors on the palate, with creamy, mousse-y bubbles. Good keeved ciders can truly have a unique texture, with a slightly higher viscosity than most ciders, combined with very fine bubbles that aren't overly vigorous.

## • MAKER: **MARTIN BERKELEY, PILTON CIDER, SOMERSET**

Keeving is an art form and Martin is a master. He makes incredibly sumptuous cider, layered in complex natural sweetness. His cidery sits in the heart of traditional British cider country, Somerset, with his fruit coming from orchards in the parish of Pilton.

This bottle is keeved and fermented with wild yeasts, but has also had barrel time, having been put into oak whisky barrels on Burns Night (a Scottish celebration, on January 25, marking the birthday of famous Scottish poet Robert Burns, often regarded as the national poet of Scotland). This barrel time adds a fascinating extra element of maturity to the cider, and gives it some micro-oxygenation, helping keep any possible reductive elements far at bay.

On the nose, there's a bit of black treacle and a soft white currant-like note, which also reminds me of sweet plums. On the palate, it has a lovely creaminess and a bit of whisky peatiness. That apple-juice sweetness comes through, being a little bit tart on the tongue. Overall there is a certain tarte-tatin thing going on, and perhaps a fudge-like sweetness, but this is far fruitier than fudge. It reminds me of raisins and baked dark sugars.

# ICE CIDER

| | |
|---|---|
| *Also known as:* | Apple Ice Wine, *Cidre de Glace* |
| *Key element:* | The juice that made the cider was concentrated by cold before the fermentation, such that the cider is high in sugar, and resembles a dessert wine. |
| *Example:* | Brännland Iscider, 2017 |

Making ice cider is another method of getting a naturally sweet cider, using the sugars naturally found in apples and their juice. But in this style, we are creating something that is more at home in the category of dessert wine.

There are two ways to go about it: the beautifully named cryoextraction and the equally seductive cryoconcentration. Most ice cider is made by the latter, cryoconcentration, with only a small amount being made the other way. Both work by the principle that the different elements that make up apple juice freeze at different temperatures; the key, water, of course freezing at 32°F (0°C). This fact allows a maker to separate out much of the water from the more flavorful elements that make up the juice of the apple, to create a far richer drink. In effect what is happening is that the maker is concentrating the cider with cold. How they use the concentrated juice that results is, of course, hugely different to the use of industrial concentrate in the mass market, and you only have to taste a good ice cider to see how otherworldly wonderful it can be.

Cryoconcentration involves freezing the pressed juice, such that much of the water in it is frozen, while the concentrated must can run free, being full of sugar and rich in flavor. This is either done by freezing the entirety of the juice, and then collecting the must that is first to thaw (the water will stay bound up in ice while this thaws first). Or, by freezing the juice to the extent that the water is bound in ice, but the must sits free, as yet unfrozen. As does ice on a pond, the water freezes to the top of the liquid, allowing the must to sink to the bottom. Only about 20–25 percent of the potential juice of the apples used is usually extracted for ice cider, containing within it the best elements of the juice. Hence, partially, why ice cider is often an expensive drink. The other approach—cryoextraction—does the freezing before the apples are pressed, while they are still on the tree. This approach mirrors most closely the manner of making of Ice Wine (known as *Eiswein* in Germany, where many of the most famous ice wines are made), where grapes are left on the vine to freeze in winter. In the same way, sun, wind, and time dehydrate the apples on the tree, giving them a sort of "cooking by cold." This concentrates their content in a similar manner to cryoconcentration, as the water content from the apples reduces. After the apples have had enough time iced upon the tree, they are pressed for their juice, now a rich must. And in this way, from the harshness of cold winter comes a drink of vibrant fruit and rich, sumptuous sweetness.

The greatest aspiration of ice cider is said to be two ingredients: apples and winter. "Natural Cold"— the cold of winter as opposed to refrigeration—is favored as the finest method. This, of course, means that

↑ A bottle of Brännland Iscider.

the place that lays claim to ice cider's spiritual home has cold winters: Québec, in Eastern Canada. The Québécois standard is controlled by legal definition, and has Protected Geographical Indication when made within the region. It sets the tempo for ice cider-making the world over, with this gold standard having many criteria, such as being made with late-harvest apples, the residual sugar level must be at least 140 grams per liter, and only natural cold can be used.

It's likely no surprise then that it's said ice cider was invented in Québec in 1990, by a gentleman named Christian Barthomeuf, who took reference from ice wine-making in Germany. But the key to ice cider-making, concentration by cold, is not new, and it would seem strange if no one had made something rather similar in the past, especially given that the natural cold of winter can do the hard part. Ice wine, for example, has been around for a long time—there are even supposedly suggestions in the writing of Pliny the Elder that the Romans used frozen grapes to make wine around two millennia ago. And where cider is concerned there are examples of similar things, such as Henry David Thoreau's essay *Wild Apples*, from 1862, which contained these words:

*"Let the frost come to freeze them first, solid as stones, and then the rain or a warm winter day to thaw them, and they will seem to have borrowed a flavor*

*from heaven through the medium of the air in which they hang."*

So the effects of such cold on apples were certainly known, and so too was the effect of such cold on cider itself: a chapter titled "Of the concentration of cider by frost," written by a Mr William Coxe of Burlington, New Jersey, published in 1817, said that:

*"I racked off two hogsheads [large casks] of good sound well flavoured cider… these I exposed with bungs out, to the severest cold of January… after a fortnight's exposure to unremitted cold, I found the cider surrounded by a mass of ice…and drew out the concentrated liquor… I mixed with other ciders to strengthen them for family use in the summer… and can truly say that it is an excellent, vinous, strong, pure liquor;… twice the ordinary strength of of good cider, and promises with age to improve to a high degree of strength and perfection."*

This is, however, speaking of concentrating the cider once fully fermented, and the process is fairly easy to imagine; say a barrel of cider is left out one winter, the water in it forms a layer of ice on the top. If the ice is removed before it thaws, the cider has been slightly concentrated. Do this a number of times over—freeze, remove, freeze, remove, etc.—and you can concentrate the cider a lot.

The key difference between this and the modern way of making ice cider, is that for ice cider today the concentrating is done before fermenting. And be in no doubt, the result of this timing creates an incredibly different drink.

Good ice cider is like nothing you've ever drunk (unless you've drunk good ice cider…). It can taste as though bursting with all the flavors of apple, a wonderful combination of tart and sweet, being both full of sugar and often acidity, too. At times its taste can be particularly reminiscent of baked apple, dark sugars, and fruit such as raisins. It is, of course, more viscous than other cider styles, and little droplets of it can seem to tuck themselves away in between your teeth, to then burst back out in flavor when touched by your tongue. While not always, and not having to be, almost all ice ciders are still, just like the majority of dessert wines.

The apples used do not tend to be the traditional cider apples (West Coast fruit). The reason being that these are often highly tannic and intense, so if you concentrate them by a factor of four or five times, they can be too much to handle, an assault on your senses! Instead, to get complexity and nuance, East Coast fruit is used; its more delicate features are intensified, and so can be incredibly complex without being overpowering.

**ANDREAS SUNDGREN GRANITI, BRÄNNLAND CIDER, VÄNNÄSBY, SWEDEN**

Brännland sits in the subarctic, on the Baltic seaboard of Sweden, where the coldest parts of winter often reach temperatures of 7°F (-14°C) or lower, providing the natural cold desired for making the finest ice cider. Their orchards are likely some of the most northerly in the world. Sitting mid-way up Sweden, only around 160 miles (260 km) south of the Arctic Circle, at a latitude on a par with Iceland. In them Andreas grows a mix of mostly Swedish, Finnish, and Russian apple varieties, including Ingrid Marie, Arome, Cox Orange, Mutsu, and Kim.

In a way, Andreas works with a combination of the two methods of making ice cider, cryoconcentration and cryoextraction, as often the apples will be frozen on the tree by the harsh Swedish winter, before being pressed for their juice, which is in turn frozen for its must. It is fermented initially in steel tanks, with a combination of wild and inoculated yeasts (inoculated yeasts where required, as the fructose levels in the juice can make things challenging for wild yeasts), and then it is partially fermented in French and Austrian oak barrels. (Andreas also makes an exquisite barrel-aged version, which is matured for a further 12 months in oak.)

Ice cider such as this is not just sweet like some dessert wines can be; the wonderful acidity it holds also gives the drink a whole other layer. It has sweetness and sharpness wonderfully balanced, each sumptuously rich. It has a lovely lot of sweet peach and nectarine on the nose, like thick, syrupy nectar. There's a slightly nutty nod, like almonds or even macadamia nuts, as well as vanilla and something biscuity on the taste, before the acidity kicks in. Then its silky thickness oozes through your mouth, kicking out mandarin-orange elements and juicy baked apples. The aftertaste, as you roll your tongue around your mouth and suck in your cheeks, lingers on and on, as the coating of its beautiful taste slowly fades.

# HYBRID

*Key element:*     There is no key element, and that's precisely the point.
                   Other than that this style is always a mix of things.
                   Reference, even method, ingredient, or style, may be taken
                   from other parts of the world of alcohol, such as wine or
                   beer, and applied to a cider. Or different styles of cider
                   may be combined, to create a hybrid blend of these styles.

*Example:*         Oliver's The Mayflower 2015

Hybrid is a hard thing to define. The dictionary definition of "hybrid" is: *mixed character; composed of different elements.* And what marks it out is precisely that, a mix of things. It is cider made with a mix of methods.

For makers who understand that our definitions of many drinks set unrealistic boundaries, this can be an area of rich pickings! For the truth is that creations such as cider, wine, and beer overlap at the edges, and are like a big Venn diagram, both in their manners of making and the tastes that can be created. You might well find a cider and a wine, for example, that are more similar in taste than most other wines from the broad spectrum that the grape can make. It's also true that while the ingredients for these drinks may be different, many of the fruit sugars being worked may be the same, as may be the yeasts, wild or cultured, doing the working. So the boundaries of many kinds of booze, different definitions though we might set, are blurry things.

It is perhaps easiest to define hybrid by example, as its possibilities are so near endless they can't be simply defined. Some examples are:

A number of makers (such as Ben Walgate at Tillingham Wines/ Starvecrow Cider, in Sussex and Simon Day at Once Upon A Tree, in Herefordshire) have been making some exquisite ciders that cross very directly into the world of wine; adding pressed grapes into fermenting cider, to create co-ferments. The key to doing such co-ferments well is a clever choice of which varieties of apple and grape are mixed, and at what ratio. Ben Walgate's saw cider made with a mix of East and West Coast fruit, fermented in qvevri on Pinot Noir grape skins, to create a dry and naturally sparkling cider. Simon Day has also been fermenting Dabinett apple juice on Pinot Noir skins, and separately also on Cabernet Cortis grape skins.

In Herefordshire, where there is a long history of hop growing, Oliver's has been infusing cider and perry with hops, creating fascinating results that play with fruitiness and bitterness. And our chosen example of a Hybrid cider comes from the same maker, Mr Tom Oliver. Its inspiration has crossed the Atlantic, and its name is The Mayflower, in reference to the ship the Mayflower that landed on the shores of New England back in 1620, the same region from which this hybrid takes its present-day cue. It blends fully fermented dry cider with an ice cider. And a number of other makers have been doing similar things; in a sense "fortifying" a cider with ice cider. For example, the collaboration Understood in Motion 01, by Ryan Burk of Angry Orchard and Eleanor Léger of Eden Specialty Ciders, that combined three-year-old ice cider with a dry cider, some from tank, some from former-use Calvados barrels.

• MAKER: **TOM OLIVER, OLIVER'S CIDER & PERRY, HEREFORDSHIRE**

I think by now Tom Oliver needs no introduction, so I will just jump straight to the cider itself: The Mayflower is a fascinating thing, being in a sense both dry and sweet, and containing a balance of potent flavors. The 2015 bottle was 9.5% in alcohol, and an incredibly rich thing. The predominant apple varieties used for it were Herefordshire Foxwhelp and Herefordshire Redstreak, with a number of other traditional cider varieties in the blend. It was fermented in four former-use oak barrels (two former red wine, one former rum, and one former whisky). Dried fruit was added to the liquid, and it was matured in barrel and then bottle for two years before being blended with an ice cider, which was partially fermented, at a ratio of around 50/50.

I would describe its perfect use as a winter drink, being hearty enough for cold winter months, and reminiscent of Christmas pudding in its dried-fruit flavors and spirituous edge. It has something fascinatingly leathery on the nose, and its sweetness conjures up thoughts of dark rum, dark sugars, and tropical fruits. It has a sort of banoffee pie, or even cheesecake, element to its taste; with fruity vanilla sweetness, then a biscuity flavor as the body kicks in, before a whack of a spirit-like, higher-alcohol taste. It's got an amazing viscosity, and a surreal pace of change, being sweetly viscous to start, before delving into its dry, slightly bitter depths. It's one that is tasted on the back of the throat, not just on the tongue. It moves about and fills the mouth as you taste it; at first the sweetness and fruitiness fill the cheeks and top of the mouth, before it billows its way down and into the back of the throat. It's incredibly layered.

# CHAPTER 7

# Drinking and Dining

The hardest part of discovering the world of fine cider is choosing which cider to drink from the many options that you have not tasted before. It is a problem shared with the world of wine; there are many different and ever-changing options— makers, vintages, etc. In wine, this is largely solved by knowledge. The knowledge of the person you are buying the drink from, but also your own knowledge, as the options are better known and most wine drinkers have a decent understanding of their own sense of taste.

In this chapter I hope to arm you with a number of tools with which to approach choosing what fine cider to drink. Of course all that you have already read will arm you fairly well in picking a good bottle, but a few extra thoughts can only help, particularly if they aim to find a simple way to answer the most important questions, or can open the door for you to perhaps the finest experience of cider of them all, that of pairing fine cider with food.

I always think simplicity, where possible, is important. Anything dug into in enough depth can become a world unto its own, or can become complex and even prove simply to be beyond true comprehension. The art of it all, in hoping to make things accessible and as rewarding as possible, is simplicity. Like finding a mathematical formula, such simplicity is no easy task, and the method itself can be surprisingly beautiful. I'm not saying that I have my numbers completely correct, and what I have written in these pages is by no means a unifying theory, but it should, I hope, help a little in opening the gates for you to the vast world of fine cider, and lend you a few paths down which to explore.

When I speak of simplicity and complexity, I think again of the world of wine. Despite the enormous complexity and detail that the world of wine has, at its simplest and most accessible, wine is often spoken of with a simple divide: *red/white, fruity/dry*. Just two binary choices that are in themselves actually spectrums. It might only be a rough fit this divide, and there are many more accurate layers beyond it for the wine drinker to discover. But it

has an incredible simplicity, and acts as the gateway to wine, making it accessible in the simplest form, and in a manner that is relative to the tastes of the individual drinker. In short, you can know what you would like, and translate this to someone else, in a decently indicative way.

← Restaurants are waking up to the fact that cider is an incredibly versatile pairing partner with food.

Where would we be without such commonly accepted devices of communication? Even if they lack the nuance desired by those in the know. So my aim is not to be more thorough on the minutiae than anyone else, but to try to simplify things for you in the best possible way. And as with the division of wine just used, I think the best way to do this is with the key factors most ciders can hold, set upon a spectrum of their intensity. In my view, the three key factors that define the cider spectrum are *sweetness*, *acid*, and *tannins*. Sweetness is, of course, far more universally known and understood. But acid and tannins are somewhat abstract things to understand, especially for the uninitiated. So the way I prefer to think of them is as *sharpness* and *bitterness*, respectively, as sharpness is a description often attached to acidity, and bitterness is often a term used for the sensation that is tannins (think of the kind of bitterness tea can have).

↑ Cider can be described by a few key characteristics.

These two criteria also roughly fit the differentiation that I have drawn in varieties, of East Coast and West Coast fruit (see page 70), as well as the more stylistic other terming for this, Old World and New World. The Old World, the domain of the traditional cider apples, tends to be high in tannins, and thus high in bitterness. The New World tends to be low in tannins and high in acidity (even if sometimes only as the perceived taste, thanks to the lack of tannins).

But sharpness and bitterness are not opposite ends of the same spectrum; they are simply two key components, the intensity or even existence of each of them can vary hugely. Old-world cider can, for example, be high in both tannins and acidity, so would be described as high in both bitterness and sharpness. And to simplify things further still, bearing in mind that sharpness and bitterness are each spectrums, running from "low in" to "high in," you could start looking at many ciders at the ends of these spectrums as "sharp cider" or "bitter cider," or where both are present as "bitter sharp cider."

These terms, bitter and sharp, might sound familiar from a thing I briefly mentioned in Chapter 3 on apple varieties (*"Cider apples can be divided into four categories called sharps, bittersharps, sweets, and bittersweets"*—see page 69) and indeed that is where they come from. So this approach, the description of bitterness and sharpness, also has a root in the varieties themselves. Therefore, in place of using *red/white* and *fruity/dry* when discussing wine, when speaking of cider you could ask this: *sweet/dry* and *bitter/sharp*? Knowing that cider can be both bitter and sharp.

I think it's worth noting also, as words can be judged falsely on their connotations, that "bitter" for example is not bad; it can be a sought-after sensation, such as in drinks like Campari, or the bitterness that can be found in beer. And sharpness is not derogatory either; in wine for example where the acidity of a white wine is often termed as "crisp" or the wonderful world of citric fruits.

If you get to know how you feel about these three factors—sweetness, sharpness, and bitterness—you will have a great tool by which to translate what it is your taste buds are after when choosing cider. You will get to know what you like in general, but also at that precise moment in time, such as you might wish to do when drinking cider with food, choosing a cider to match a specific dish. So let's take a look at what goes with what, what cider suits what season, and goes with what food.

→ Cider often has a summer connotation, but can be wonderful drunk year round.

# A CIDER FOR EVERY SEASON

Just as apples are the fruit of the orchard, so too is cider in some ways the fruit of the sun: it is the sun that makes these apples grow and creates the sugar that becomes this wonderful alcohol, yielding the glorious complexities of its conversion. And so fittingly, it is cider that is the perfect summer wine, being summer's most beautiful libation and companion; coming from the sun of one summer and often ready to be first drunk under the sun of the summer the following year.

But just as all seasons have their part to play in the making of cider, so too do different ciders suit different seasons. Their varying properties tend to appeal to our palates at different temperatures, and cider beyond the mass market is truly a thing that holds a year-round drinking calendar, for all seasons, not just summer...

In spring and early summer, the succulent or crisp delicacies of perry and sharp ciders, which are often youthful like spring and lower in alcohol, fit wonderfully to quench those first true thirsts of the returning sun. Such sharp ciders can pair perfectly with spring lamb, with a sharpness like the vinegar in mint sauce, and at times herbaceous flavors such as rosemary. This is also the time that keeved cider from the previous season may start arriving, and its sweetness and low alcohol can make for easygoing joy.

In summer, it is simply a matter of taste. Things that sparkle can be the most wonderful accompaniment to the heady haze of a hot day, keeping things light, but nearly all cider can suit. This is the time of plenty, and it's down to your taste buds at the moment as to what will suit best.

In fall/autumn, as the days shorten and our bodies begin to demand warmth, more bitter ciders can come into their own, warming and feeding the richer requirements of the palate, all the while fortifying you with often greater levels of alcohol.

In winter, the sweetness of ice cider, keeved cider, and "fortified" hybrids can work against the cold, but also the rich depths of a dry and full-bodied cider can give the alcohol and fullest flavors comfort against winter's chill. Both of these, the sweeter and the driest end of the spectrum, can pair beautifully with the dishes of game season, in all their gamey grace.

# HOW TO SERVE CIDER

Where temperature is concerned, for drinking cider, I usually like a bottle chilled to around 50–54ºF (10–12ºC), but it really depends on the specific cider or perry. Some can benefit from colder temperatures, such as Pet Nat or Traditional Method ciders, especially on a hot day, whereas some (still ciders in particular) can benefit from warmer temperatures, even right up to room temperature, as this allows them to open up, to breathe, and to display their fullest flavor. Still ciders (see page 142) can also sometimes benefit from being poured into a carafe before drinking, aerating them and opening up their flavors further still.

For glassware, something with a stem is usually best, particularly if the cider is chilled, as holding the stem will stop the cider being warmed by your hand. The shape of the glass is also a factor as the best shape will work to enhance the nose of the cider. The glass should camber upward, closing in slightly as it rises. This concentrates the smell to give you the fullest nose. As taste and smell work together, and humans can detect taste through their nasal cavities, getting a good nose can give you the fullest taste of a drink—if you drink a cider direct from the bottle, your mouth will cover the opening giving you less of a smell of the cider, and as a result less taste.) Smell is a most incredible thing—we don't need to see a thing to smell it, simply detecting particles from it in the air. And it is not a thing that can be written

down by definition in a dictionary that we can all read; smell is an archive of memories, a dictionary unique to each of us. Everything we smell and taste we are comparing to things we have smelled and tasted in the past, stumbling upon reminiscences and trying to make them conscious. It is no wonder that people describe cider and wine by virtue of other flavors, common things that most of us know, having had them on our own taste buds and up our noses.

← Stemmed glassware is the go-to choice for drinking fine cider.

# HOW TO PAIR CIDER AND FOOD

I genuinely feel that the one rule with pairing any drink with food is that you cannot truly know if it works without trying that specific pairing. You can gain an intuition and settle upon some general rules, but still things can perpetually surprise you.

Guessing what will not be terrible together is one thing, and you can roughly approximate, but the true skill of pairing lies in both the cider and the food being better for the combination. Sometimes one will enhance the other, but at a loss to itself; for example cider can go wonderfully with hot, spicy food, cleansing and calming the palate, but sometimes the taste of the cider can be lost in the process. When both drink and food enhance the other, both sing, and the experience is wonderful. It is a nuanced thing to find such a pairing, and when done to enough detail it is of course relative to the quirks and appeals of each individual's palate. Some may prefer one pairing to another; we each have our own sense of taste after all. But in general, most people will agree on good pairings; the argument will come over which is best! So let's run through some of the things that I have discovered, and then we'll look at some specific examples of pairings, done with some wonderful customers of mine.

I have come to believe that fine cider pairs with food more broadly than any other kind of alcohol, wine included. Its versatility with food comes from its versatility as a creation, providing fascinating rich fruit flavors, sharp acidity, tannic bitterness, sumptuous sweetness, deep dryness, floral flavors, savory tones, or even spice, to name but a few of its many possible facets.

I have also come to think that one of the main ways for a drink to enhance a dish is for it to cleanse the palate as it is tasted, such that you get the fullest flavor from each bite of food. So you don't want either the drink or the dish to accumulate over time and become dominant in your mouth; instead each should perpetually reset the other, giving your taste buds the greatest journey possible.

One of the key factors for pairing cider is fat, primarily because, as a general rule, acid cuts through fat. Tannins also come into play, as they bind to proteins, such as those found in many fatty foods, meaning both will free up the surfaces in your mouth, cleansing your palate for the next bite. Salt is said to enhance tannin, meaning bitter ciders may seem extra bitter with salty food, but sweet ciders often pair very well with salty foods; the classic example is salt with chocolate, and such a combination of sweet with salty brings out the fruitiness in the cider and at the same time the savoriness of a dish.

There are certain tastes that I often come across in cider, so I am going to give you a few examples, to describe some of this in action. Commonly occurring can be notes of rhubarb, gooseberry, under-ripe fig, prune, rose water, or slight orange and mandarin notes. I have found that wild yeast ferments with East Coast fruit (low tannin, high acid) can often develop a certain smoky wet-slate taste, that can come across as though the cider has been Bourbon barrel-aged, even though it hasn't. And sometimes acidic ciders can seem to have a very "green" taste, that reminds me of very under-ripe plum, and the smell of spring plants like cow parsley. Keeved cider can often be on the creamy side of things, with a silky texture from fine bubbles. Dry cider made with traditional cider apples can have elements of spice, pine resin, leather, straw, or even lactic blue cheese notes. And some of the finest ciders I have tasted from Devon can seem to have a certain note that reminds me of salt licorice—I am still not sure where that comes from...

Perry can be more floral, archetypally with notes of elderflower and grapefruit. It can work wonderfully as an aperitif, as well as paired with white fish, and of course cheese, particularly with goat's cheese. Cider, in its many different forms, can of course fit most wonderfully with pork, that archetype of its companions. But take the principle of food with a fat content and you can apply it widely: cured meats, pâté, cheeses, shellfish, and game all often pair wonderfully with cider. Protein-rich pasta can also make for a great pairing.

More savory ciders can pair beautifully with vegetal dishes, their fruitiness also plays wonderfully off the acidity in many salad dressings, adding that burst of sweetness that can suit salads well. As too can sharp ciders, pairing with such things as raw tomatoes. Roasted vegetables that develop sugars as they cook can also combine well with drier ciders, as can the earthiness of mushrooms, a delight with the tannic end of the spectrum. Mushrooms can also combine with cider, holding earthy flavors, such as Traditional Method ciders can. And then we have dessert—need I mention fats again? Desserts with fruit are, of course, ripe territory for pairing, and I won't mention cheese again, but the cheese board is a shoo-in... Then, after dinner, keeved cider and perry can be like a dessert wine in their own right, making for a wonderful digestif, as of course does the king of this role: ice cider.

Often the most pleasing pairings are ones of local significance; being a

↑ As awareness of fine cider grows, restaurants are starting to treat it more like wine.

dish from ingredients that are in season and exist naturally in the region where the cider is made. Such as the pleasure of drinking cider from orchards near the coast, paired with mussels, as in Devon (see page 176). Or a rich tannic Herefordshire cider, with Herefordshire beef or Herefordshire pork. Herefordshire is also home to a number of wonderful cheese-makers, whose cheeses can make for wonderful pairings. And then there are other ways you can go about things, such as using a Pet Nat or Traditional Method cider in the place of a sparkling wine in cocktails; I work with some award-winning bars who use cider in their concoctions.

# PERFECT PAIRINGS

At Fine Cider, we supply some of the UK's best restaurants with cider to pair with their dishes. Here are some of my favorite pairings, which can be used as a template for cider-matching.

**• PASTA AT WANDER**  STOKE NEWINGTON, LONDON

*Dish:*        Goat's curd and fennel pollen cappelletti with fermented pepper water and coriander oil

*Cider of choice:*  Little Pomona, Old Man & the Bee 2016

I don't think you could find a finer local restaurant, one that would be worth a journey but that you're grateful to have close by, so you can easily visit again and again. Its influences are mixed, shaped by its wonderful Australian chef and owner, Alexis Noble. They include Asian elements from her Australasian upbringing, influenced of course by the cuisine to the north, as well as pulling in Italian elements, such as some exquisite pasta. They bake bread in-house, make their own ricotta, and have a wonderful drinks list, unlikely to be found anywhere else. It is a creation and operation manifested so

wonderfully from one individual; Alexis's personality shapes it all, not that it doesn't take a great team to pull off, of course.

The proteins in pasta can pair well with more tannic ciders, and in this cider we have both a good lot of tannins and a good bit of acidity. The filling of the pasta gives it rich bursts of flavor, the sharpness of the cider going well with the sharp side of the goat's curd, and the mature barrel-aged flavor of the cider combines well with the latent richness of the fig and sage.

← Pasta can pair well with tannic/bitter cider.

## • FISH AT LYLE'S SHOREDITCH, LONDON

*Dish:* Grilled dried mackerel with fermented gooseberries, lovage, and chervil

*Cider of choice:* Oliver's Yarlington Mill 2016

I love lunch at Lyle's; they keep the priorities right: seasonality reigns supreme, simple combinations of ingredients, all of exceptional provenance, skillfully combined in dishes you are unlikely to find anywhere else. You always get the feeling that everyone involved in each area of the restaurant, from the pastry chef to the person pouring the coffee, is in eager pursuit of the depths of their own field, and not simply because it is demanded, but through their own innate personal desire. In short, they all fit, and it's fascinating to think upon all of their futures. Yet Lyle's keeps things casual; there's no false fancy or irritating embellishment, they prioritize the taste of the food on the plate. As the saying goes, it takes a lot of effort to make things look effortless… Luckily, it's not just me that thinks so—in 2018 Lyle's joined the list of *The World's 50 Best Restaurants* at number 38, making it one of the four British restaurants on the list. Such lists can be contentious things, but in my view Lyle's deservedly being on them is not.

Mackerel is an oily fish, and this oil can contain a good bit of fat, so the acidity of the cider cuts through it, cleansing the palate. But as well as being oily, mackerel can be both wonderfully flavorful and have a near creamy texture. The more robust, even slightly herbaceousness of the Yarlington Mill stands up to the richness of the dish, as well as accompanying the herbs well. The sharpness from the gooseberries acts to bring out the fruitiness in the cider, so both enhance the other accordingly.

→ Acidity in cider will cut through oil and fat.

## • SHELLFISH ON THE BEACH AT FIND & FOSTER DEVON

*Dish:*          Mussels with fennel, cider, and leeks

*Cider of choice:*   Find & Foster, Methode Traditionelle 2016

As you'll know by now, Find & Foster is based is Devon, on the south coast of England, and it was home to one of the most wonderful pairings of cider with food that I have ever had. The combination itself, the locality of the food and drink, and the beauty of the setting happened upon its shore. I have mentioned that local connections between a drink and food can make for a great pairing, or, as it's often said in wine, "what grows together, goes together." This pairing is a great example of that observation; it is the maker's own, coming from and enjoyed in their own landscape, the locality of their life, and the food that surrounds them.

It's always a particularly wonderful kind of warmth that a fire can provide, especially on a fall/autumn day when temperatures drop sharply as soon as the sun goes down. Pair this with mussels from the very sea from which you are sat just a few steps away, cooked on the same fire that is keeping you warm, with cider in the sauce and also in your glass, that was made not many miles up the road, and the simple life can be incredibly refined and incredibly rich.

The fennel flavors bring out the fruitiness in the cider, and the minerality of the cider plays wonderfully off the saline nature of the shellfish. The cider's bubbles cleanse the palate between tastes, and the cider itself is not so dominant as to overpower those more subtle mussel flavors.

→ Cider here is used in the cooking, as well as being the pairing.

## • SUNDAY ROAST AT THE APPROACH TAVERN BETHNAL GREEN, LONDON

*Dish:* Spring lamb served with roast potatoes, green beans, carrots, Yorkshire pudding, mint sauce, and gravy

*Cider of choice:* Starvecrow Pet Nat 2016

The Approach Tavern is, in my view, the perfect city pub. Its wonderful landlord, Mr Samuel Brookes, has shaped a thing of old charm and new quality. A combination of black lacquer, to last a century, and Dijon mustard color its walls. Large rectangular windows let the last of the light in from the residential street outside, acting as a reminder of the waning of the day and its surrendering to the night. A large and gated outdoor area, tapered by a canopy to keep those drizzly days away, allows you to pass easily between inside and outside.

The backs of pew-like seats rise high, and stools cluster around tables. The timber of the floorboards shows their wonderful wearing, worn like a point of pride as to the steps that have passed over them. The lives lived, the tipsiness gained, and the tales told in the wider lives of those who have had this place as their sanctuary—this is the very essence of the pub.

The food is always wonderful here, true to the classics of the pub yet done that bit uniquely, and what could be more classic than the Sunday roast. I love lamb with dry East Coast or sharp cider, the lamb heightens the fruitiness of the cider, and the cider cuts through the fat of the lamb in the mouth, cleansing the palate. The texture of lamb is also rather dense, and the bubbles of this Pet Nat cider act as a fascinating contrast, being so vibrant and light.

→ A dry cider can go perfectly with a Sunday roast.

## • DESSERT AT THE MARKSMAN
HACKNEY, LONDON

*Dish:*        Custard tart, followed by ewe's milk ice cream

*Cider of choice:*  Brännland Iscider 2017

↑ Replace the traditional dessert wine with an ice cider.

The Marksman is something very unique. It was the winner of the Michelin Pub of the Year 2017 (there were around 48,000 pubs in Britain in 2017). The downstairs has the bar and dark wood of a historically refined local, and upstairs is a restaurant that is fitting for its Michelin accolade; luckily, both floors serve their exquisite food.

I have worked with Jon and Tom, the two chefs and owners, since the day they opened (we actually had our first tasting when it was still a building site), and I remember one time coming through the door to find them both sat at the bar, bedecked in their chef's overalls, reading through old cookbooks. Old is not an exaggeration. Some dated back to the 18th century or earlier. They were the people who made me realize just how much the history of the British Empire has shaped food and drink in Britain to this day. And they look to take inspiration from old recipes and ingredients that were more often used upon this isle before it set so aggressively out across the seas. So I thought what better to pair with their food than a thing of equal uniqueness, that is shaped so hugely by the place of its making in the world—Brännland Iscider, from Sweden. While this ice cider can pair wonderfully with rich and fatty meats, such as duck breast, it will always be exquisite in a dessert role.

The Marksman's ewe's milk ice cream is wonderful stuff. Ewe's milk is higher in fat than cow's, and makes for rich ice cream, with a slightly funkier complexity than normal ice cream (a little reminiscent of the "goaty" side to a good goat's cheese). Here we are combining cold ice cream with chilled ice cider, but the two both give a lot of flavor at such temperatures, slowly transitioning from the flavors of one to the flavors of the other and each opening up as it warms in the mouth. The custard tart also has a role to play, where the acidity is enough to cut through the fats of the custard and the pastry, with the ice cider's sweetness highlighting the tart's more savory side. Both the tart and the ice cider show off complex "baked-sugar" flavors in the cider; it's a world of glorious sweetness that never becomes cloying.

# CHAPTER 8

# The Future

Of course, no one knows what the future holds, so I am simply going to offer a few thoughts and speak of a few hopes: most of all, I hope for more makers, all over the world. As we've established, it takes all the efforts of many people combined for things to truly evolve. I'll be fascinated to see what their collective efforts culminate in, concisely guided by the undercurrent of things, as niches form and regions rise.

The future of cider has started to arrive, but what comes next? What hopes will become realities, and what realities will change cider forever? One thing that has become incredibly clear these past few years, is the truly international nature of what is going on in cider. So many different cider-making regions, both new and old, are asserting their unique identity, and this shift in cider, from the industrial to the more exquisite, is happening on the global stage, not just in little old England. This makes sense in many ways when you understand cider and its similarities to wine—by which I mean the similarities in how both are made when made well. Where differences of origin, terroir, and place present different possibilities, and create beautifully different things by their very nature. So it seems to me that the way the trade winds are blowing, and the weather system of cider is settling into place, we are simply going to see these different regions become better known, their identities more settled and the word spread globally.

What is the best cider that any particular region can produce? This can be a tricky and complex question to ask and is knowingly (or unknowingly) a question being evermore answered by the many wonderful cider makers at work around the world. And I think this sense of variety that exists between different regions has begun to, and will continue to, extend beyond major boundaries and into the smaller scale. Scotland is a great example with all that has changed there in cider-making just in the last few years, and whilst still so young as a country on the cider map, it is forming an identity that is by no means a carbon copy of somewhere firmly established like Somerset or Herefordshire. Increasingly, it won't just be the differences that exist across an ocean that are known, but also state borders and even county lines.

There is also a lot of youthful vigor in cider right now, more than ever before, and how it evolves further on the stage that has been set will very much define the next few decades. Great cider has more devoted fans than ever, and these fans have enabled it to grow from being the preserve of those who make it, to a scene in its own right. But as the earlier paths forged by craft beers and natural wines show, the next stop will almost certainly see the wider public getting on board. And exactly how this happens, what styles or formats will have wide enough appeal to truly make this breakthrough, will turn what is currently a possibility into an established reality.

There have already been the first hints that the behemoths that are the mass-market cider brands are taking note of how cider from fine cider makers is growing in strength as a category. And here in the UK, for example, we have even seen changes to the law on cider duty, with relief for small producers being introduced. The small cider makers' ranks have been growing, the big cider makers have been thinking... What ultimately will form between these two opposite ends of the spectrum? Is it some long-time missing new middle market? Or a broader definition that encompasses both?

But either way, there is definitely still the complex task of getting a simple message across to the wider public. To educate them as to what cider has become in recent years, and what it can become in the future. What exists, and what could exist. What is known to them, and what they are missing out on. I say simple message because that is what it will take; just as the word "natural" is so powerful when put before the word "wine", in presenting people with a clear narrative of a point of difference, one that appeals to modern values (even if the technical side of the term is anything but simple!).

I do feel that you can never undervalue practicality, even when the actual thing you value about something is anything but practical... It might take a romantic spirit and some great storytelling to truly share the nature of the thing in order to highlight its virtues, but there are always questions of practicality that dictate where this story can be told. And I'm always mindful of how naturally wine seems to work as wine, and beer as beer (the first favoring big bottles poured into small glasses, the latter big glasses and small bottles or cans), and how incredibly different these norms are, for just two alcoholic drinks. The prevailing format can change in big ways over a short

↓ → Give a creative maker access to the right fruit and the right tools and the results are alchemy.

time, as the Magners cider boom in the UK in the mid-2000s attests (see page 53), but still a groove is found and becomes the norm, for a while at least. So what does the groove of good cider, in a form and format that pervades the public consciousness, potentially look like?

Environmental factors relating to packaging are certain to change things over the coming decade for alcohol in all its forms, as a price to be paid beyond one of just monetary value becomes increasingly weighted. Reuse, not just recycling, will have subtle and lasting effects, as a spiraling, not just circular, economy gets going. For every style of alcohol it will pose questions; what is more practical and what is less so for these new conditions? Other factors, such as electric vehicles that are charged from sustainable energy supplies, or even more elaborate possibilities way further down the line, such as driverless vehicles, could make the cost of moving things around for the purpose of reusing them far more economical; which makes you wonder if just as the way that the cost of renewable power has overtaken many fossil fuels for value, we could now reach a situation where reusing things such as packaging, becomes more economical than creating single-use packaging each time. If transport becomes so cheap as to offset production costs, it is not only morally better, but economically better too.

I am going off at a slight tangent here... but it does makes me wonder if our future might not see packaging downplayed in some ways, or at least evolving with the focus shifting more towards the

← Landscapes shape the flavors in fine cider, the terroir/ locale giving each maker something unique.

liquid itself, whilst packaging increasingly serves a different prerequisite, powered by these environmental concerns. That may seem optimistic, in our modern world, one seemingly obsessed with visual language, but I simply mean that where the visual language is very prominent (such as in branded drinks packaging) it may shift further into our digital world, where the identity of a product or brand manifests itself ever more in pixels, while the physical product itself holds new priorities. Perhaps...

Having talked a little about some possibilities for the future of cider, it feels like a good idea to go back to the start, to the future I imagined when I wrote the first edition of this book in 2019. To quote here from my conclusion, and to reflect once again on the nature of making the finest of ciders:

*"I imagine the regions in different parts of the world, each making cider that is like nowhere else; all exquisite, all simply different. Even the best makers in each region becoming known for their house style. As this is a fascinating thing about the best makers, each has to make choices; they can't replicate what another maker does because there are too many options, too many choices of details too diminutive to control. How do you tread a path of routes beyond comprehension? You make choices based on wider principles. It's a reflection on the maker, the choices they make, that subtle sense of values and what they wish to achieve in their most nuanced persuasions. It's a whole lot of betting, placing a bet that they won't even know the outcome of until the darkest months of winter have given way to the crisp blue of middle spring, at the earliest. And it's not a bet where you know the choices, where there is a list of runners, set options to choose between. It's a form of betting where you know the only way to improve your odds is to learn from your failings and come back year after year, making subtle changes to improve your intuition. They are both gambler and competitor, in conditions that are ever-changing".*

Now, I consider cider's strengths—the variety and depth it can have, virtues so familiar to us when it comes to wine. It occupies a strange territory, somewhere between wine and beer, with exquisite cider often that bit lower in alcohol content than wine, and also with a more affordable price tag. I start to imagine, dare to hope, that we will see more cider being served by the glass; free-flowing, as beer often is in Spain. And in the short term, in the more immediate future, will will see a more abundant variety of different ciders, from more places, in more places; a celebration of provenance and variety, both local and broader. There is a new world of cider emerging, and the more that new makers appear on the scene, the more there will be to explore. It is this exploration that changes tastebuds, that makes once-loved, mass-market drinks taste dull in comparison to the new cider territory now becoming known to us. And your tastebuds need no prior knowledge, they take from their own experience, they are their own sensory dictionary.

I also still ponder the continued prevalence of still and dry wines. We have seen an increase these past few years in still ciders becoming better known—their dry depths better appreciated, for both their food pairing possibilities and competitive price point in comparison to wine. Whilst on the sparkling side, it's hard to ignore that over the recent decade, the dominance in the market that Champagne had always enjoyed, has increasingly been challenged by sparkling wines from other regions and of alternative styles, from Prosecco to Cava, Pet Nat to Crémant; so will the finest sparkling ciders join this fold in due course?

So whilst writing, once again, about what the future holds for cider, perhaps it's best to think about the liquid itself, the uniqueness of this fascinating drink—what it really is beyond economic forces alone and to understand its true nature through all we have covered and learned in the pages of this book. As it's these basic principles from which all paths originate. Cider makers must take lessons from the past, muse on the multitude of variables, embrace the challenges they face, consider the options that present themselves, the sheer variety of possibilities that cider actually has as a drink, being a thing that can be made in myriad ways.

Every little labor the cider maker undertakes, the time they spend, the nuances they understand and the boundaries they break contribute to the final outcome. It is so evident to the maker (and the merchant) that all of these parts set the stage, define in subtle ways what the wrangling of economic forces will eventually form; just as wine by its nature ends up poured by the glass from big bottles, and beer by its nature often ends up pulled by the pint, there are these subtle differences at play that will butterfly-effect their way to shaping what results on a vast scale. What can be done, what can't be done, and what will triumph, all has its roots here.

↑ A new dawn has risen on cider; it's exciting to see what the future will bring in the fullest light of day.

# INDEX

Page numbers in *italic* refer to
the illustrations

# ACKNOWLEDGMENTS

The list has grown quite a lot since the first edition, and to name just a few:

Andy and Hamish of the Tate (book launch among many things); everyone who helped us through a certain pandemic (such vast kindness that can never be repaid); my partners and colleagues at The London Cider House; and the individual efforts of Sam at Noble, Matt and Coombeshead, and Debbie of Wild Wine; all people who have shaped my words, and there will be many more to come in the next few years…

Pete, Cindy, and everyone at my publishers, who made this thing become real.

The incredible eyes of James Moriarty and Olivia Estebanez, who went to the ends of the earth and the extra mile, in the early hours and the cold of the night.

My makers (mum and dad) and the brother who dreams big.

All of the efforts of Aga Ciemiega and Theo Cobb, who make so much possible. And the past labours of Emily Boyfield, Aqsa Qureshi and Freddie McArdle.

The cider-makers: Tom Oliver and Jarek; James Marsden; Polly and Mat Hilton; Beccy and Sam Leach; James and Susanna Forbes; Ben Walgate and Steeve Reeve; Martin Berkeley; Andreas Sundgren Graniti; Simon Day and Sally Booth; Alex Hill; Martin Harris; Ben Slater; Ryan Burk; Eleanor Léger; Dennis Gwatkin; Paul Stephens; Adam and Dani Davies; Barrie Gibson; Jörg Geiger.

I'd like to thank every single customer we have had, but will take this opportunity to single out a few who I am particularly grateful to for all of their support: John and James, and the family of Lyles; Charlie, Nomi, Freddie, and everyone else; Trevor Gulliver and Fergus Henderson (Ms & Mr St John); Kitty, Linda, and Max; Samuel Brookes; Alexis Noble; Jon Rotheram and Tom Harris; Andrew Downs and Hamish Anderson; Jackson Boxer; Rob Simpson; Tom Allen; Wai-Ting Chung; Charlie Mellor; Jen Ferguson and Glenn Williams; Holly and Brad Carter.

Thanks to Sebastian White and Eva Kellenberger (Kellenberger-White), as well as BCMH, Luke Watts, Henrike Dreier, and Simon Whybray, for all of their graphic design. And thanks to all of the authors noted on the reading list.

I would also like to thank Claire and Adam (for the sanctuary they provide); Angie; Alice Lascelles; Alistair Morrell; Matthew Albone; The BLCC (for easing a tricky summer); Martyn Sharman; Sam Wilkin; Elizabeth Pimblett; the YBFs.

# READING LIST

*The Apple Orchard*, Pete Brown
*Inventing Wine*, Paul Lukacs
*Early Days of Cider Making*, E.F. Bulmer
*Reinventing the Wheel*, Bronwen & Francis Percival
*The Story of the Apple*, Barry Juniper & David Mabberley
*The History and Virtues of Cyder*, Roger French
*Bursting Bubbles*, Robert Walters
*Ciderland*, James Crowden

*World's Best Cider*, Pete Brown & Bill Bradshaw
*The Book of Pears*, Joan Morgan
*Bulmer's Pomona*, Ray Williams
*Golden Fire: the story of cider*, Ted Brunning
*The Book of Apples*, Joan Morgan & Alison Richards
*Empire of Booze*, Henry Jeffreys
*The Evolution of Everything*, Matt Ridley
*Keeping Bees*, Paul Peacock
*Three Centuries of East Herefordshire Farms and Families*, Jean Ila Currie